At War
with the
Big Dogs

How One Man in Need of a Job Started

a Billion Dollar Industry

By

CHUCK MASEK

ISBN: 978-0-9998712-6-3

AUTHOR'S NOTE

As I look back on my life, and the twist and turns it has taken, the one common thread I can observe is how providential those twist and turns were. Although I would go on to invest in several other companies, for me Vanguard was, and will always be, the high-water mark of my career.

I feel overwhelmingly grateful and privileged to have served with the men and women who, although bloodied and bruised, soundly defeated the Big Dog Kingdom! It is these Vanguard warriors that I wanted to honor as I sat down to write this book. Also, I hope that readers of this incredible tale who find themselves facing overwhelming odds or obstacles will take comfort knowing that the fight does not always go to the Big Dogs.

To God be the glory!

— Chuck Masek

For the only person in this world whom I ultimately trust—Marge, my wife, my best friend, my one true love. Without you, none of this would mean anything. Without you, I am nothing.

When I pass from this life into the next, my last thoughts will be of you.

Table of Contents

Prologue

There is nothing impossible to him who will try.
— Alexander the Great

Everybody loves a success story, a tale of how someone fought through all the obstacles in their way and were able to experience the life they had only dreamt about. Such stories remind us that there is usually a price for everything we achieve. In the famous phrase by Winston Churchill, it is all about blood, sweat, and tears.

There is a little of each of these in my story.

My tale contains lots of unexpected twists and turns on the path to finding security and contentment. Often when I thought my dreams were just in sight, everything I was depending upon collapsed in front of my eyes. And when that happened, time and again, I had to depend upon my faith, and upon the love and support of my wife and best friend, Marge. With her help, and God's strength, I survived another day, and I defeated the Goliaths that stood in my way.

Mine is a kind of David and Goliath story.

Recently I was sitting on my porch with a cold beer in my hand as Marge was bustling about the house, preparing party favors for a celebration with our grandchildren. I gazed out over my property and thought about how I came to be here. I see the majestic old oak tree that stands undaunted before me, which could have been felled by one of the storms that frequently blew through, yet remains firmly rooted in spite of the punishing winds and rain that have felled so many trees before. I am like that oak. After all I have endured, I am still standing strong.

I cannot help but think about the combination of hard work and God's grace which brought me to this moment. I am happy, content, and successful. Not too many years ago that was not an assured outcome. I have stumbled and fallen many times along the way, reminding me that I am as unremarkable as the next man. In truth my failures are part of my story. How they were redeemed is what drives it forward.

I hear barking coming from somewhere in the distance. Judging from their insistent sound, the dogs responsible for it are big and strong, with sharp and threatening teeth. I am reminded of a time when I had to face down the "Big Dogs" that threatened me. But now I can barely remember the fear of being bitten. I am now at peace, and the barking is just part of the cacophony of the evening. My thoughts drift back toward the past, as the leaves stir in the branches of that oak.

I feel the breeze gently caress my face, and I remember…

Part I

Basic Training

The world breaks everyone, and afterward, some are strong at the broken places.

— Ernest Hemingway

CHAPTER 1

THE MAGIC WORDS

No pressure, no diamonds.

— Thomas Carlyle

Even before I stepped into the elevator, I felt the pressure in my head. It wasn't a pounding that had increased in intensity throughout the day, as had been happening for the past few months. I had watched cash—first just a trickle, but more recently a cascade—bleed out of the company. It wasn't caused by being overlooked or dismissed by my colleagues. It wasn't even the result of a blinding fury triggered by the realization that I was probably not ever going to be paid what was owed to me. On that day back in 1984, it felt like my head was going to explode if I didn't get some answers from my business partner.

It was four floors up to Dick Isel's office, a distance I usually covered by the stairs in just over a minute. For someone like me, who thinks, eats, walks, and does everything at a speed most people consider breakneck, stairs wouldn't—couldn't—have gotten me in front of Dick quickly enough to figure out what was going on. So that afternoon, although I have always been somewhat claustrophobic, I jammed the elevator button more than once, thrust my hands into my pants pockets, and then rocked intently on the balls of my feet as I waited for the floor numbers overhead to illuminate in turn.

When I burst into Dick's office, no faces lit up. Dick's brother Jeff was there, as was Jim, the CFO. Although I was visibly agitated, no one registered outward surprise at my entrance. Maybe they didn't know what I wanted. More likely, it was because they didn't care why I was there. Before any of them had the opportunity to come up with another excuse for why I still hadn't been paid the expenses I was owed, I took the initiative.

"Where's my money?" I blurted out, staring at Dick, who started squirming in his seat.

His response came out as a slow sigh: "Chuck …" It was as if my asking for what was rightfully mine was somehow disappointing to him; as if by phrasing an adequate response, he would be admitting responsibility for blowing me off. So instead of speaking, he offered me a seat.

I couldn't possibly take the chair he gestured to, his arm outstretched and his palm facing upward. I was too agitated, so hot under the collar that it took all of my energy—and I had a considerable amount of energy back then—to keep from launching myself over his desk, grabbing him by the shirt collar, and allowing my rage to fully manifest itself.

"I can't keep waiting," I thundered instead. "I know you've reimbursed Mike's expenses, so where's mine?"

Dick gave me a tight smile. I can't imagine what I must have looked like to Jeff and Jim as I stood there, overflowing with incomprehension and anger. Dick looked decidedly worn out. "Let's give it another couple of weeks, why don't we?" he finally sighed. Then glanced over at Jim.

It was at that moment I realized all three of them knew precisely why I was there. They were all involved in—complicit in—the decision to pay out other people's expenses and not to reimburse mine.

"Sales are looking good," Dick continued, the smile withdrawn and replaced with faint hope, "so why don't we ..."

I stopped listening at that point. I knew sales were looking good. I was a big part of the reason *why* sales were looking good. From independent sales representative to regional sales manager to national sales manager—how could my rapid ascent have been possible if I hadn't come of age as a salesman in this very company and ultimately grown to guide its sales strategy? I'd been there at the beginning. I'd helped turn things around in the Tampa Bay territory.

As I thought about all the money I had made for this company, which was led by a man who had just screwed me over, the pressure in my head gave way to another sensation: lightheadedness. The sound of the blood rushing in my ears was almost deafening. The force of it behind my eyes was nearly blinding. My legs became so weak that I nearly collapsed into the seat across from Dick.

Then Dick stubbornly crossed his arms and leaned back in his chair—as if I had just marched into his office and demanded that he reimburse me for something he hadn't promised, something I hadn't rightfully earned. He behaved as if I were just another sales rep pressuring him for something I didn't deserve.

* * *

It had been several years since I'd first sat in the purchasing department at Alachua General Hospital in Gainesville, Florida, as a relatively inexperienced salesman. That day, I was dressed in my three-piece suit and tie, with my company badge pinned to my chest. I remember looking over at the somewhat disheveled man seated next to me, measuring him up before mentally dismissing him: *Not much to see here.*

I pointed at my badge as I spoke to him, telling him I sold for Travenol Labs, drove a company car, and, with my expected bonus, would make close to $25,000 that year. When I asked him what he did for a living—a question men commonly ask each other when making small talk—he said he was an "independent sales rep." I didn't know what it meant to be an independent sales rep, but his appearance suggested that it couldn't be a very profitable job.

I glanced down at the Rolex on my wrist as I asked him, more out of politeness more than actual interest, "So what do you make, being an independent sales rep?"

"A buck and a quarter," he replied.

He said it so casually, I thought for a moment he meant he made a dollar twenty-five. It took a beat for me to realize that the somewhat sloppy salesman sitting in the plastic chair next to me was making six times the amount of money I was.

My Travenol badge suddenly felt like it was sliding right off me, slipping down the front of my sleek suit jacket before landing at my wingtip shoes.

* * *

Some months later, at a medical devices trade show, I met two men who would reroute my career. At Travenol, we sold IV start kits, which had all the necessary elements for a single-use IV. While an increasing number of hospital IV teams were asking if we could customize the kits, Travenol only sold standard kits and had no interest in offering customization. The men I spoke to that day, Clay Page and Jeff Isel, represented Sterile Design, a competitor who offered sterile, custom-procedure kits and packs to hospitals. I remember thinking that Jeff and Clay were on to something with their custom kits, even before they said the magic words: "We're looking for independent reps."

Later that same year, after I had moved my family to North Carolina and blown through the twenty-thousand-dollar profit made from the sale of our previous house, we were almost out of money. My income as an independent sales rep was commission only and it didn't come close to supporting my family and my business expenses. I was barely hanging on, and I knew I couldn't do it for much longer. So, when Bill Frisbey, my trainer from Travenol, moved me back to Lakeland, Florida, in February 1981 and gave me the Tampa Bay territory, it felt like a reprieve.

Two years later, I was ready for a new challenge. By that time my commissions were healthy once again, but Sterile Design's offer to hire me to work for them promised even greater financial security. So, my wife and I sold our house in Plant City, Florida and relocated to Sharon, Massachusetts, where I became the regional sales manager for the Northeast.

When Dick Isel—who had started Sterile Design with his brother Jeff and my future partner Tom Howard—wanted to bring me back to Florida in 1984 as national sales manager, I wasn't going to look a gift horse in the mouth.

Dick signed a promissory note for the twenty thousand dollars of my personal money I would have to use to cover my relocation expenses. The note stated I would be reimbursed as soon as I got back to Clearwater. A promissory note was good enough for me because if I wanted the job, it had to be done that way.

Our home in Plant City had been purchased by a doctor who'd secured a good deal for himself—he could move in immediately but close on the property in one year's time. This left us with no proceeds from the sale, and no home to return to. We made the decision to move to Palm Harbor, which was close to Sterile Design's corporate headquarters in Clearwater.

But the doctor in the Plant City house ended up defaulting on the mortgage, and we were forced to take it back. Now we were left paying three mortgages every month, since we had two unsold former houses.

Adding to the financial hardship was a showdown I never saw coming—one that had nothing to do with real estate.

* * *

As I stood in Dick's office and mentally replayed all of the ways he had tried to get out of paying me my agreed-upon moving expenses—first by stringing me along, then by avoiding the conversation, and ultimately by outright telling me he would need more time to come up with the cash—I felt like I was about to completely lose my cool.

And then he said it.

"Listen, Chuck." Dick thrust himself forward in his chair and pointed a finger at me. "You'd better keep your nose straight if you still want to be an employee here."

And then I erupted.

It wasn't so much what I heard as what I saw: Dick's finger, thrust out menacingly at me. As if I was asking him an unfair question. As if I wanted something from him that I hadn't earned. As if I was sniffing around for money that wasn't owed to me under terms that had been agreed upon by the man in front of me.

"Employee?" I spat out. "*Employee*? You and I both know I'm a part owner of this company, you son of a bitch. Without me, you—" Here I paused to look at Jeff, then at Jim. "Without me, *none* of you assholes would have a company, so don't give me that bullshit. You *needed* me back here, Dick. So give me what you owe me, or I'm going to kick your ass!"

I may have taken a step forward with that last threat, but no one made a sound. For the brief period of time I continued to stand in that office, my breath shallow and my chest heaving, there was a molten rage surging through my body.

Then, in the same way I had entered Dick's office without warning, I turned and walked out.

Back in my office I would likely have appeared outwardly calm to anyone who saw me, but resentment was roiling inside me. I paced back and forth, back and forth, my ire rising to an intensity that made me feel like I was going to lose my mind. *How could he call me an employee when I'm an owner?* I raged inwardly. *A minority owner, sure, but I'm part of the team. I'm not just some employee!*

And then, as if a valve had been opened and the pressure suddenly released, it hit me. I could keep looking back at what had just happened, or I could start looking forward and *do* something about it. I could stand still or I could move forward. Either way, I was done with Sterile Design.

I dropped into my chair and exhaled, releasing a breath I hadn't realized I had been holding. *Well, that didn't go well Chuck,* I thought, laughing softly to myself. *But this just might work out.*

I picked up the phone and dialed the number for DeRoyal Industries, Sterile Design's largest competitor. On the second ring, my call was answered. As calm as glass, I asked for Steve Stephenson.

"Hey, Steve," I began when I heard his upbeat voice on the other end of the line. "Seems like you guys could use some help with your custom trays. You looking for someone?"

CHAPTER 2

TENDER WOUNDS

All wars are fought twice, the first time on the battlefield, the second time in memory.

— Viet Thanh Nguyen

As soon as he sees the knife, my twelve-year-old brother Ted is out of there. My heart is pounding in my throat, but I don't follow him down the hallway and into our bedroom. It is only when I'm older that I will learn about the fight-or-flight instinct and how the sympathetic nervous system reacts to life-threatening situations. On this night, however, even when Ted takes off running, my body keeps me anchored in my seat. I may be sitting stock-still, frozen in fear at the dinner table, but my mind is racing through scenarios— not of what could happen to me, but of what my younger brother might be doing in our room. He could be standing with his back against the door, as if to shield himself. Or maybe he's under his bed, his arms clutching his knees as he berates himself for not grabbing the baseball bat that is kept propped against the dresser. I, at age fourteen, have no way of knowing what Ted is doing because, unlike him, my body's reaction to the stress and the danger we have faced together so many times, makes me incapable of running.

My father is by and large a good man. He is a brave man, honest and courageous, and he generally treats other people with kindness. He takes us fishing on weekends. We join him on long drives, the warm wind whipping through the car's open windows and against our cheeks. He often invites our friends along too. They laugh in the backseat with us as Dad takes corners too fast and opens up the throttle on the back roads. By all estimations, the man I'm named after is decent and tenderhearted. Later in life, he will even develop his artistic skills. But he is also, in many ways, a man broken by the experiences of his life.

Yet I share more than my name with my father. We also have in common that we have been robbed. The very thing my father takes from Ted and me on these nights is what was taken from him years earlier on a distant battlefield—innocence.

Ted is probably wondering what's happening out at the dining table. He's likely expecting me to rush to the relative safety of our room. He must be worried because long minutes have passed since the knife was brought out. He has to be imagining that I am thinking, *I'm going to die tonight, at the hands of our father.*

Ted has a tendency to be clumsy and spill things. This time, it's a nearly full glass of milk which he's knocked over. Since this is just another average night in the Masek household, a fight is all but certain. The only unknown is where on the scale of 1 to 10— yelling to actual bloodshed—tonight's fight will land.

Dad had warned Ted that his glass was set too close to the edge of the table. When Ted's elbow caught it, it fell as if in slow motion, the swell of milk rising out of it before splashing over the sharp and shattered fragments of glass like a heavy coat in the stifling July heat. A few droplets had spattered on Dad's cheek. For a moment, time stood still.

Ted should have recognized that as Dad slowly wiped his face with the back of his hand, that now was the moment to run. I too should have known that there would be no coming back from this moment. Whatever happened was going to happen, and none of us—not even me, who was sometimes able to cajole Dad back to an even keel—could do a single thing to stop it. When it came to our father, Ted and I could never predict the things he would overlook and the things he wouldn't. If Dad had been a mean bastard all the time, his behavior could at least have been predictable, and we'd have had some consistency in our lives. As it was, we never knew what to expect from him.

Without warning, Dad thrust himself to his feet, the force of his sudden movement knocking over his chair. He stood there without saying anything, his expression contorting. It was as if he were trying on a mask that didn't quite fit, and that by clenching and releasing all of the muscles in his face, he could adjust it properly.

When the mask was finally secure, he didn't blink. Not once. Not when Ted, stammering, apologized for making a mess. Not when I set down the fork I was still holding, signaling that I was ready to help Ted clean up. Not when my mother sighed and rose from her seat, lifting her plate of half-eaten fried chicken and carrying it in one hand as she sauntered into the kitchen.

Ted's head was bowed, his fingers fiddling with the edge of the tablecloth. My mother turned on the water in the kitchen sink. My hands went limp in my lap and my mouth clamped shut. I knew this was one of those things my father wouldn't be able to laugh off, one of those times I wouldn't be able to manipulate his mood with a well-timed wisecrack and pull him back from the brink. This wasn't a summer storm that was going to pass over our house without making its impact felt, suddenly changing course or losing critical mass. This storm was about to unleash its considerable power on us.

My mother's clanging of the dishes disrupted the eerily calm air. She wasn't angry. She wasn't frustrated. She wasn't even dismayed. She was simply looking to have some fun. She let out another sigh that, if you didn't know her, would have seemed innocent and even playful. If you didn't actually know my mother, you would probably like her. The mean streak that had opened up in her after a wounded childhood now ran a mile wide. My dad knew exactly what that sigh of hers really meant. It taunted him for his weaknesses. Her sigh was a test: would he shrink back, or would he *do something*?

If Kathryn Masek had been the type of woman to worry about her appearance, she might have stood with her back to the dishes, one ankle crossed over the other as she leaned against the sink and held a nail file to her hand. Her fingers might have been bent into her palm as she smoothed her nails. But no matter what she did or how bad the fights got; my father's face would always be a menacing storm cloud while my mother's would remain an undisturbed blue sky. We all knew that when you pierced her calm, you unearthed something dangerous which cut deep and took its time to heal.

The chair was still lying on its side when my dad's face finally settled. My mother's sigh had also dissipated, and she was no longer pretending to do the dishes. She was facing the dining table, and her gaze was solidly fixed on my father.

Is that it? her piercing eyes communicated to him.

Dad didn't move.

That's the best you've got?

His chest heaved. His fists were balled at his sides and his knuckles were starkly white. But his feet were fixed in place. As long as he didn't move, he had some control of himself. As long as he didn't move, he could withstand her goading.

As always, my father had no real chance of withstanding my mother, so he turned on his heel and stalked to the kitchen. He threw drawers open, their contents clanging and clattering like the dishes had done moments before. He was searching for something Ted and I instinctively knew we didn't want him to find.

While Dad was preoccupied with whatever need had overcome him, my mother slowly crossed her arms. Apart from the small smile that played at the edges of her lips, her face didn't give anything away. She didn't raise her voice. She never did. Without speaking a word, she could get my father to do all the yelling and shouting. In fact, she could get my father to do whatever she wanted, even if it meant that she was on the receiving end of the rage she had provoked.

It was only when Ted and I saw him hulking in the kitchen doorway, knife in his hand, that Ted finally ran. I heard his footsteps fall frantically away from the table and down the hallway.

My father held the steak knife like his Marine Corps–issued combat KA-Bar, low and close to his side.

If, as my father came undone yet again, my mother *had* simply been filing her nails, this would have been the moment when she'd blow a lazy puff of air over her curled fingers, diffusing the filings that had collected along her nail beds.

* * *

My father had fought in the Second World War and had been part of the Battle of Okinawa. This fierce battle against the Japanese in the Pacific theater took countless lives on both sides. The battle on Okinawa was a horror show. Driving rain and mud so deep that it often prevented the soldiers from retrieving their dead, whose bodies decayed and created a stench that permeated everything. And then there was the constant bombardment of shells and what sometimes devolved into hand to hand combat with Japanese soldiers who refused to surrender and would fight to the death. Sometimes the Japanese would use innocent civilians as human shields. The ruthlessness of the Japanese sparked a similar kind of ruthlessness in the Marines who fought there. The psychological effect on the American soldiers who survived was a syndrome called "battle fatigue," which is similar to what we refer to today as PTSD (post-traumatic stress disorder). The battle took its toll on every soldier, including my father, who was psychologically scarred in ways I don't think he ever fully understood.

He didn't really like to talk about it much, but I remember him occasionally telling the stories of what he had experienced. Once he was kneeling in the mud with the stock of his Browning automatic rifle hard against his right shoulder. Staring down the sights of the rifle, he fired in three-round bursts toward the place he and his fire team had been told the enemy was located. He felt fatigue in the muscles of his forearms, caused by the constant vibration of the rifle. But with his left elbow over his knee, he felt steady. He had been taught the position in boot camp the year before. It already felt like his time at Parris Island Marine Corps Recruit Depot had happened in another lifetime and belonged to someone else.

But there were some important things the instructors hadn't taught him, a few crucial truths they couldn't teach any of the "men." They were really just boys, seventeen, eighteen, and nineteen years old—who fought and died alongside him. He would later find out that there were another eighty-eight thousand Marines and soldiers with him out there in the Pacific. Only after the war had ended and he was safely back in the US would he learn that fifty thousand never made it home.

"Last magazine!" he shouted as he pulled the remaining rounds from the magazine pouch hanging from his cartridge belt.

"Get 'em yourself," came the answer from the other rifleman who shared the sector with my father. My father moved nearer to him, firing all the while.

Knowing his fire team had all sectors covered, my dad broke his position to move to the rear. Thanks in part to his youth and the adrenaline charging through him, there was no stiffness in his joints. Life's many small disappointments had not yet set in and slowed him down.

They say if you hear the *whiff* of a round, it's not too close. But if you hear a *whizz*, it's nearby and you're in real trouble. My father didn't hear a *whiff* or a *whizz*. Neither did the lance corporal.

The lance corporal—kneeling momentarily in the exact position my father had held for *days*—heard nothing. The round didn't pass that lance corporal at all. Instead, it stopped in his throat and made a sound the likes of which my father had never heard before, and only ever would hear again in his nightmares. The lance corporal, who could have come from any family in any state, collapsed atop his Browning, bled out, and died in my father's place.

Later, the fire team came across a body in a rice paddy, lying face down. My father tried to blink away what he saw. It was an image he could have effortlessly captured on canvas if he had carried a paintbrush with him instead of a Browning. But back then, he wasn't an artist. Instead, he was forced to carry a rifle. He turned away from the mangled body half-buried in the endless expanse of mud.

"Shoot him!" the sergeant barked at my dad.

The Japanese soldier had lain unmoving in the wet and dirt for several minutes. *Surely he can't hold his breath this long*, my father thought. He pulled the Browning to his shoulder, his eyes staring down the sights. Finger on the trigger, he hesitated.

He didn't need to look at the sergeant to feel the rifle pressing into the flesh of his forehead.

"You ever hesitate again," the sergeant growled, his finger on the trigger, "and I'll shoot *you* first."

Then he fired two shots: one into the dead man's back and one into the dead man's head.

* * *

When my father lunged, steak knife held high in his clenched fist, I could have sworn I saw my mother's smile broaden. The knife found the back of the sofa, where the fabric was pulled taut over the wooden frame. There was a *pop* followed by the sound of tearing as my dad sliced downward. Again he thrust the knife into the fabric, *pop*, then ripped down. Again he thrust. Again he sliced. When there was nothing left to stab and the back of the sofa was shredded beyond all recognition, he moved around to the front, ripping into the cushions and throwing them aside one by one as they were destroyed.

By now the smile left my mother's face, but her arms remained crossed. She was so transfixed by the way my father's rage was being acted out that she clearly didn't remember I was still seated at the dinner table.

* * *

Though Ted grew up to believe our mother had never protected us, I have never felt that way. There is no doubt that her actions aggravated my father's PTSD. But the one positive thing I learned from her was how to be a fierce competitor. This has helped me again and again.

I was never athletic or muscular; actually I was rather small for my age. But mentally, even as a boy, I was tough. The way my mother treated me ensured that I would be.

"Chuckie," she would say to me when we lived on Wildwood Drive in Charleston, South Carolina, "I bet you can't run out to the mailbox and get the mail back to me before I count to ten."

I would run outside while she waited, mentally counting the seconds in time with my breathing and the pumping of my arms and legs. When I made it back to the house, out of breath every time, my mother would say "eleven" or "twelve," taking the mail from me and turning her back. No matter how fast I ran, I could never make it back to the house before she got to ten.

Years later, when my parents were living near me and I saw them somewhat regularly, I once mentioned this recollection to my mother. "No matter how fast I ran, I could never make it back in time."

Typically emotionless, my mother simply said, "I didn't count—I just called out a number when you opened the door."

I was flabbergasted. "Why, Mom?"

Shrugging, she answered, "I wanted the mail quickly."

Mom used to take us out in the car, but unlike Dad, she didn't drive for pleasure. One day, Ted and I were riding along with her. We were in the backseat with the windows down, throwing pennies out the window. I don't remember if we watched the pennies bounce alongside the car, or if we just enjoyed throwing them outside.

"Are you boys throwing pennies out the window?" Mom asked in a flat tone.

Neither Ted nor I said a word, our hands dropping to our laps.

"No worries," she said. "Let's go get a candy bar."

I looked at my brother as if to say, *Silence is golden.* One time after we'd gone to the movies, Ted had ended up paying dearly for lying about eating from boxes of popcorn left by earlier moviegoers. This time, we thought we had gotten away with throwing those pennies.

My mother pulled up to the small general store, parked the car, and reached into her purse. Out came a nickel. Holding the nickel out to me, she said, "Go get a candy bar for yourself and Ted."

In those days, candy bars were large and cost a nickel—with a penny tax. I went into the store, but quickly learned that I was a penny short. I went back out to the car. Ted and my mother's faces were both expectant, but for very different reasons.

"I need a penny," I explained.

"No problem," my mom said. She put the car in gear. "We can go back along the road and see if we can find one of those pennies that you so easily threw out of the window."

We didn't get a candy bar that day, and it didn't surprise either of us. Mom was tough, and stone-cold. If she said you were grounded for five days, you weren't going outside for a full five days. On the other hand, if Dad said you were grounded for five days, you could usually work on him and be hanging out with your friends by the third evening.

Despite her harsh lessons and impassive demeanor, people generally liked Mom. No one knew why she took such pleasure in winding Dad up and provoking him into an argument, even if it meant that Ted and I would take the blame—and the hits. She would do it even when it meant that *she* would take the hits. Perhaps even more strange was the fact that my mother didn't ever lose *her* temper. To this day I don't recall my mother, not even once, raising her voice at me or Ted. She had other ways of making her point.

We didn't know if the things that happened in our family also happened to our friends, but we knew well enough not to mention what was going on at our house to anyone else. One time I asked a buddy at school if his parents ever fought. He told me they didn't, and I responded, "Oh, did they tell you to say that if anyone asked you?" We understood that our mother would never lose her temper with us the same way we understood we were to keep our family business within the family.

One time I asked my mother why she never got angry. "Chuckie," she replied, "if you are right, you don't need to lose your temper. If you're wrong, you shouldn't lose it. There is never a reason to lose your temper."

* * *

My father's rage, though, always burned hot and fast. This particular time the storm blew over when he ran out of cushions to slash. No television set would be thrust through the window this evening. No wedding rings—that we would later spend hours on all fours looking for, when his regret set in—would be hurled into the field behind the house. On this night the mask slipped only briefly, and he quickly became my father once again. The knife dangled from his fingers as if equally exhausted.

"Well," Mom said, uncrossing her arms and returning to the dishes that were languishing in the sink, "I guess we'll need to replace that sofa."

My father didn't respond. When his breathing was steady, he looked at me and then glanced down the hallway toward the back bedroom, where he now realized Ted was hiding. Unlike other times, Dad didn't take a bowl of ice cream to my brother to express his remorse. He was so drained and devastated by what he had done that he simply sank to the floor and dropped the knife.

I didn't need my father to tell me he was sorry. I never did. I *knew* my father was sorry. I had known it after the hundreds of fights I'd witnessed before that night. And I would know it after the hundreds more before I turned eighteen and left home. *Almost a thousand fights done*, I told myself as I watched my father slowly rise to reposition the tattered and torn sofa cushions. *Only a few hundred left. I can do that.*

CHAPTER 3

LEFT TURN IS THE RIGHT TURN

I took the one less traveled by, and that has made all the difference.

— Robert Frost

In GI parlance, Crete has just two seasons: dry and tourist. For young airmen like myself, who were stationed on the Mediterranean island in the late sixties and early seventies, and who found ourselves languishing during the dry months, the tourist months of April through September felt like a long-awaited promise. During that time of year, hordes of young ladies from Europe, America, Canada, and Australia descended on Crete. But on cold and windy January nights, all we GIs had to keep us warm were the memories of tourist seasons gone by.

During my first year in the air force, I was a model airman. Prior to my service, I had attended Brevard Junior College (now Eastern Florida State College) in Cocoa, Florida, enrolling in August 1968 with a draft deferment. After three months of too much partying and not enough studying, I came to realize that college wasn't for me. So, I withdrew with the registrar's assurance that there would be no grades recorded on my academic transcript. I was also assured that my information would be sent directly to the draft board. Two weeks later, I enlisted in the air force. Therefore, I was in basic training at Lackland Air Force Base in San Antonio, Texas, when my draft notice arrived.

After basic training, I found myself doing time: first at Keesler Air Force Base in Biloxi, Mississippi, for Morse code training; then in Texas, at San Angelo's Goodfellow Air Force Base, for non-Morse code intercept training. Finally, I spent another month in technical school, closer to home in Pensacola, Florida. I had the same job Johnny Cash had during his time in the Air Force. Whereas the "Man in Black" had been stationed in Germany, I found myself headed to Iraklion Air Station on the Greek island of Crete.

The base was located in north central Crete, about fifteen kilometers or "klicks" away from the city of Heraklion. Iraklion Air Station had only been in use for about fifteen years by the time I got there. It fell into disrepair after its closure in 1994, and is now home to a marine park that includes the Cretaquarium, Greece's first large aquarium. But during my time, the station served as a top-secret security service facility dedicated to snooping electronically on the Soviet Union and its Eastern Bloc allies.

On Crete, for the first time in my life, I found consistency and routine. Earning my own living was an important part of that security. Although I had held jobs back in the States, I'd only worked, as teenagers often did, to save up for the things I wanted—things like a new surfboard with a single balsa-wood stringer. Flipping burgers for ninety cents an hour all summer didn't give me independence. What I gained was the satisfaction of hard work and the sense of accomplishment from *earning* something.

Don't get me wrong: I wanted to quit that summer job many times. One evening, despite the hazy late-day heat, a woman dressed in a fur coat had stumbled drunkenly through the parking lot. Her bagged burgers swayed in her hand as she tried to negotiate her way back across the road, only to be hit by a car. I ran outside in my grease-stained apron to where she lay sprawled on the sidewalk. There was no blood, but I heard her moan. Someone standing behind me said, "Pull her dress down." I wanted to quit that day, but I hung around long enough to save the ninety dollars I needed to buy the surfboard.

I hadn't known it at the end of that summer, when I was finally able to buy the longed-for surfboard, but my days on the waves were numbered. On Crete, I could no longer surf, as there are no surfing waves on the Mediterranean. Although my pay as an E2 wasn't much, the Air Force provided the only thing I truly needed, counterintuitive though it may seem: my freedom. Looking back, it makes sense that this feeling of independence wouldn't and couldn't last. Military service, I quickly came to realize, wasn't exactly synonymous with autonomy.

For my first year, I had no problem following orders. I'd grown up under my father's military-style rule, after all. *Yes, sir* and *No, sir* and "whitewall" haircuts were nothing new to me. But on Crete, the combination of the dry season and the restrictive, patriarchal Greek culture became too much. Before long, I was hanging out with guys who were bad influences on me…and I ended up making a lot of bad decisions. As the saying goes, "If you lie down with dogs, you get up with fleas."

The general rule on the air station—likely intended to keep us airmen out of trouble—was that single GIs had to live in the barracks. This meant that not only would I exercise, eat, hang out, and otherwise live with the same group of guys, but I'd also be a roommate with some of them. I desperately needed space and decided to take the risk and live off base. My decision to rent a two-room apartment off base—really a portion of a local family's home—was an easy one to make. It was also cheap, with the monthly rent paid in cash over a couple of shots of ouzo with my landlord.

I purchased a Volkswagen van. I don't know how a gray van with "DEUTSCHLAND BUNDERPOST" painted on the side ended up on Crete, but I took it as my good fortune that the German post office seemed to have no further use for the vehicle. For thirty dollars and three cartons of cigarettes, the value of which was about sixty dollars, I had the van painted green.

Keeping it gassed up was another issue entirely. Both cigarettes and gasoline were rationed. Unlike most of my fellow airmen, I was driving on and off base every day, sometimes several times a day. I quickly realized that if I wanted gasoline, I needed to learn how to use the local black market, despite the risk that doing so posed to my military career.

After a few failed attempts back in the States, I had finally quit smoking. At that point in my life, going cold turkey was the hardest thing I had ever done. But the extra income I made from selling my cigarette ration for ten times its value on the black market made it easy to stay on the wagon and not start smoking again.

Late in the afternoon on January 19, 1971, Bob Keyt and I got off work and were itching for a little action. Bob was driving his VW van, and I was sitting in the passenger seat as we headed toward the base gate. When we arrived at the guard shack, we gave a casual wave in the direction of the guard, and he motioned us through.

We'd already decided to take a right turn toward the city of Iraklion for a night at the bar. We were smack-dab in the middle of the dry season, so no tourists would be around. And the Greek girls were too well-chaperoned to be out unaccompanied. On those dry-season nights, a dollar spent at the NCO club's "nickel night" could go a long way, as could a good meal off base.

At the last second, though, Bob turned left and said, "Let's go to Mike's instead." Mikalis, or "Mike" as he was known to us GIs, ran a hole-in-the-wall café in Hersinossos that catered to tourists and US servicemen. At Mike's we could talk freely, because locals didn't frequent the café.

GIs were forbidden from wearing uniforms in town, but not because we were considered unwelcome on Crete. The Greeks were never rude or aggressive toward us. Although I didn't understand it, the climate at the time had more to do with local Greek politics, and the current dictator resisting the Communists, than any American presence on the island. Even when I was downtown and saw an American mail truck on fire, the burning top peeled back like a tin can, I couldn't comprehend why anyone would blow up one of our mail trucks.

As Bob's van moved east along the highway, neither he nor I did much talking. There wasn't much to talk about. We knew all of the tourist girls were back in their respective countries, and our evening was going to consist of sitting out on Mike's patio and watching a full moon meet the Mediterranean Sea as we gobbled six-egg omelets and knocked back a few beers. So, when we saw something in the distance that looked a bit like the silhouette of a woman, we didn't exactly trust our eyes.

* * *

With two world wars in the rearview mirror, European countries had come to view the reestablishment of international travel, especially by youths, as a way for nations to come together and encourage understanding. During the summer of 1971, therefore, thousands of young Americans descended on Europe in search of adventure before returning to their studies in the fall. The book *Europe on $5 a Day* was their Bible. It provided the secrets they needed for how to eat, sleep, and get around on the cheap. And those who followed its suggestions would meet other young people pursuing the same path. All a traveler needed was a few dollars, some flexible plans, and an open mind.

By the time Marge arrived on Crete, she had been away from the States long enough to miss peanut butter. It wasn't that she couldn't find any European peanut butter that compared to the American kind; Marge couldn't find any peanut butter at all. Certainly not in Matala, an ancient Roman colony on the south coast of Crete. However, a few days earlier she'd been fortunate to meet a GI who told her that if she came to the air base, he'd be able to get her some peanut butter from the commissary.

Unluckily for Marge, but fortuitously for me, the GI who'd made the offer was on duty and unavailable when she arrived. So she'd left empty-handed and was still craving peanut butter as she hitchhiked back to where she had been staying in Agios Nickolaos. Maybe she would find some peanut butter in Israel, where she was headed on the next leg of her journey.

When Bob and I realized that our eyes were in fact not deceiving us, and that we were definitely looking at a young woman in a red coat walking along the road, we knew we had to see if she needed help. She was alone and dusk was rapidly approaching. Something had to be wrong for her to be out there on that lonely stretch of road by herself.

It's true that Bob and I were concerned, but it is also true that just before Bob pulled over to the side of the road, he and I had flipped a coin to see who would make the first move on the mystery girl, who we by now had guessed was an American.

When Marge got in the van, I wasted no time putting my coin-toss victory to use. I gave her all of my best lines. Though at nineteen I looked like I was sixteen and behaved like I was twelve, I was feeling pretty good about my chances.

That is, until Marge spoke.

Though I can now attribute it to her practical and matter-of-fact nature, and not to judgment or frustration, at the time—and after all of my best come-ons—I couldn't have imagined that the first words Marge would speak to me would be, "How old are you?"

Her stoic demeanor made it clear that she saw right through my immature antics. Although her impassive expression might have stopped a smarter man in his tracks, I was too stupid to be deterred, so instinctively I said, "How old are *you*?"

"I'm twenty-one."

"Well, I'm twenty-two."

As if she was thinking, *Well, that's a bunch of BS*, she replied, "No, you're not."

I was caught off guard by how transparent I must've seemed to her, but what she said next stunned me. Though she wasn't in any way confrontational in how she suggested it, she said there was one way we could easily put the issue to rest: "If you're twenty-two, let me see your military ID."

Bob was cringing with embarrassment for me, but I was incredulous. Who does this girl think she is? Does she not know how the game is played—and that her role is to play along?

Maybe it was because of how I had been raised, but I always anticipated manipulation. I was constantly on guard for confrontation. There was no doubt I was frustrated with Marge—

this girl who not only saw through what I was trying to do, but made me feel stupid for thinking I would get away with it.

I was also intrigued.

The time we spent together that evening was unlike any I had shared with anyone before. The thing about Marge, on that day and to this very day, is how easy she is to talk to—how easy she is to be around. She just makes it effortless. No games. No pretenses. No wonder my juvenile pickup lines got me nowhere with her!

Back then, feeling the stirrings of something I didn't understand, yet knowing I had to make sure Marge didn't walk out of my life forever, I clung to my tried-and-true behavior. I continued to make an ass out of myself most of that evening.

I really liked her. And at the end of the evening I *really* didn't want her to leave. I wanted to see her again. In fact, I was desperate to see her again. I just needed an angle. So, when she said goodbye, I said, "You'll come back."

She looked at me.

I stared back at her, hoping my expression didn't betray me. I said it again: "I know what's going to happen here. You'll come back."

At Mike's the following night, I was barely aware of whether the moon was out at all. My thoughts were fixed on this girl who had unexpectedly swept into my life, and who I feared was about to breeze out of it again. I could do nothing but worry. Because I was wrong, and it hadn't happened. Marge hadn't come back.

When I first arrived at the café, I could hardly breathe with the anticipation of seeing her again. As the night wore on, my chest was almost heaving from the fear that I wouldn't see her again. *I've blown it*, I thought. *I shouldn't have tried so hard to be cool— why did I have to try so hard to be cool?*

And then, just like that, she was there.

A friend who was already in Israel had written to warn her that there were bullet holes in the kibbutz walls. Marge had decided to stay longer on Crete. She would stay for another six months.

Though I only came to realize it years later, after my immature stupidity and temper had waned, Marge continued to be there for me. She became the steady force that I needed.

During our early days as a couple on Crete, Marge was also there for Reefer, the dog I bought when I moved off base. I named him for the reefs I wasn't surfing. I loved Reefer enough to pay half a month's salary to bring him back to the States later that year. The way Marge treated Reefer was different. Maybe it was a result of her not being allowed a pet when she was growing up, but when Marge laid eyes on that mutt, it was love at first sight.

She didn't fall for me as quickly as she did for Reefer. I had my good qualities. I was able to recite some poetry from memory, like her father had done. I could also get my hands dirty working on a car's engine. But I wasn't always smart enough to know when to keep my mouth shut. Even Reefer figured it out before I did. After being petted and walked and groomed by Marge for months, I swear that dog looked at me one morning and said, "If she goes, I'm going with her."

Thankfully, Marge has never gone anywhere. All these years later, I find myself saying to people, "Should Marge ever leave me, I'm going with her."

Marge and I returned to Crete thirty years after we first met on that dusty stretch of road. We didn't recognize much. Hersonissos was decidedly not as we remembered it. A Hard Rock Café, large water park, and several five-star hotels had replaced the sleepy village we'd known. I guess it really is true what they say about not being able to go home again. With Marge at my side, though, I quickly came to realize that I don't want to and will never need to look back. With Marge at my side, I am right where I should be—at home.

And if not for her love of peanut butter, I would never have found it.

CHAPTER 4

TWO SCRAPPERS

"Nana korobi ya oki."
Fall down seven times, get up eight.

— Japanese proverb

Marge and I left Crete separately. Returning to the States in August 1971, servicemen were getting such abuse from the public over the Vietnam War that I changed into my civilian hippie clothes in the airplane bathroom (after claiming my free ticket at the counter while dressed in uniform).

Marge joined me at my next duty station near Shreveport, Louisiana. She stayed with my parents in Gainesville, Florida, for a little while before coming to Barksdale Air Force Base. Her original intention had been that while she was in Florida, she would enroll in college and also work to save some money. When my service ended, I planned to join her in Gainesville, where we would both attend college. I hadn't told Marge much about my parents and their relationship while we were together on Crete, but it wasn't long before she was crying under a tree in my parents' backyard after enduring one of their arguments. She was shell-shocked and knew that she couldn't stay with them.

Unlike the situation with my parents, and to a lesser degree with her parents' relationship, Marge and I were allies from the moment we met, united against all hardships that would come our way. Marge arrived in Louisiana with six hundred dollars in cash she earned working at the Howard Johnson's in Gainesville. I had three hundred and fifty dollars a month from my salary as a buck sergeant. So, we bought a car for three hundred dollars, paid seventy-five more for the first month's rent on an apartment in the low-income neighborhood of Bossier City, and purchased a bed for another hundred—as well as a squirrel monkey for twenty-five bucks. A few weeks later, the car burned up in the driveway. Marge seemed to take even that in stride, which helped me learn how much it would take to piss her off.

It was more of the same on the day we got married. My friend Kirby Bromley forgot to bring flashcubes for the camera. As a result, there were no pictures taken during the actual wedding ceremony. And the chaplain charged us twenty-five dollars to open and shut the base chapel doors! Kirby and another friend, Rocky Malme, served as witnesses and brought their girlfriends along to see Marge and me get married. Marge's hair was long and flowing, soft waves falling from a center part, and she wore a high-collared, long-sleeved white wedding dress/hot pants combo. I thought she looked stunning, though I'm sure the chaplain had a story to tell his buddies when the ceremony was over. The only pictures we have of the day were taken when we arrived home. All that didn't much bother Marge.

Even her response to my marriage proposal was typically Marge.

"Why don't we get married?" I asked.

My soon-to-be-bride's reply? "I can think of a lot of reasons."

This was not the answer I had expected. Of course, by then I should have expected that the response I received would be logical and grounded in practicality. Echoing our first conversation on that Crete road, I found myself pretty miffed anyway. (Though, with hindsight, I probably could have phrased the proposal a bit better than I did.)

"Well," I said, "we aren't going to live together unless we are married." Despite the volatility in their relationship, I never doubted that my parents loved each other. As a result, I had always wanted to have a wife and family of my own.

Marge just smiled. "Okay," she said, "let's get married."

Forty dollars and two gold bands later, we were husband and wife.

To make extra money, Marge and I worked evenings together at the first Pizza Hut in Bossier City. Like me, Marge has never been afraid of hard work. By age sixteen, in her small North Dakota hometown, she had essentially been farmed out by her mother as low cost labor for a pregnant woman and her six children.

I cooked pizzas and Marge waited tables. Now *that* was an exercise in patience for me, and probably why to this day I tip 25–30 percent for good service. Watching demanding diners make her run to get them this and that, only to tip her with the loose change in their pockets, got me really hot. I couldn't stand to see someone so nice—because Marge is a genuinely nice person—get treated badly for no reason at all. This unwarranted mistreatment, I recognized, also bothered me because it paralleled how Marge had been treated in her early life. Her experience had been brutal in a different way from my childhood, but it was no less painful.

* * *

Marge believes that everything she needed in life had already been formed or learned in her childhood. Living in a town of roughly five hundred people, Marge knew almost everyone. The benefits of these relationships, and the unconditional love of her father, Ralph Dotzenrod, helped her to develop a strong and independent spirit in spite of mistreatment and neglect by her mother Erma.

From her father, Marge gained a great love of the land and literature. Ralph, who received only 8 years of formal education, went on to memorize many pages of Shakespeare, Edgar Allen Poe and other poets while driving his tractor in the fields. One of Marge's favorite childhood memories is of her father entertaining the family with dramatic poetry recitations at the dining room table.

Marge's mother, was born into a South Dakota farm family, the seventh of fourteen children. Life was harsh on the plains, and children were viewed as free labor. Erma was artistically inclined, talented at both drawing and music, and she longed to develop this side of her nature, but was continually thwarted by the myriad duties assigned to her at home. Through persistence on Erma's part, her parents had allowed her to be the first of her siblings to attend high school. She went on to attain a teaching certificate, which enabled her to teach elementary school children and subsequently move to California. There she met Marge's father. A year later they were married and moved to Wyndmere, North Dakota. In this small-town setting, Erma once again found herself stifled creatively, this time burdened by the unrelenting demands of motherhood.

Marge was the second of six children born to her parents, and Erma was delighted to have her own little brood to bring up in her own way. In her household, there were no "spic and span" requirements. Instead, each child was taught to play the piano and encouraged to experiment freely with science and art projects.

Of all her siblings, Marge was the only one who fell in love with music—to such an extent that she has devoted much of her life to developing her skills. She studied voice, piano, and music theory in college, and over the years has learned to play the piano, organ, flute, oboe, recorder and most recently, the ukulele. Among the delights of Marge's life was singing for nine years in a ladies' barbershop quartet, "Sweet Spirit". For many years, she has managed "The Beachcombers," her own variety show group. For her early education in music, Marge is forever grateful to her mother.

Yet Erma's neglect of some basic household duties eventually caused a rift between Marge and her mother. As Marge grew older, she compared the conditions in her home to those of others in her community, which is likely why Marge participated so enthusiastically in 4-H and Future Homemakers of America, where she was taught by other mothers how to cook, sew, and keep a home. In fact, Marge rose to become a state leader in FHA, and at her high school graduation was presented with the Betty Crocker Future Homemaker of America award. On the other hand, Marge has no memories of her mother ever taking her shopping for clothes or caring for those kinds of needs. Instead, Marge sewed her own clothes or went shopping alone with money given her by her father.

One particular incident marked the beginning of Marge's awareness of her personal appearance. As she tells it, "At about age six, I was walking downtown with a girlfriend from across the street, when a gentleman approached us. He looked at my companion and said to her, 'What a pretty little girl you are.' Then he turned to me and said, 'And you, too.'

"What I remember most is that I completely agreed with the man's observation of how beautiful my friend looked. She had on a clean, fresh dress, socks and shoes, and her curly hair was fixed up with a pretty matching bow. She surely did look like a doll!

"Then I looked at my own ragamuffin appearance: mismatched clothes, dirty fingernails, and bare, dusty feet. I realized that my hair was cut short and not properly combed. It was an early turning point in my consciousness that there was a standard by which people were judged, a standard of which I had previously been oblivious.

"Since my mother already had three little ones younger than me and was pregnant with her sixth child, I knew even then that if any changes were going to be made, I would be on my own to make them."

Marge's attempts to improve her life must have been a frustration to her already overwrought mother, and was surely one of the factors that led to Marge bearing the brunt of Erma's hostility for the rest of her years at home. During one of her rages, Erma said accusingly to Marge, "You have a black heart."

By the providence of God, these words didn't demoralize Marge. On the contrary, protected by an inner shield that had developed over the years, Marge clearly remembers thinking, *What kind of mother would say that to her child? There must be something wrong with my mother.* A conviction grew in Marge that when she had her own home, she would cultivate a different dynamic with her own children and husband.

And there's no doubt that she has been successful. To this day, I remain in awe of the wife Marge is to me and the mother she is to our four children.

* * *

Along with the job at Pizza Hut, my nights were consumed with the college classes I was taking on base. When I was honorably discharged from the air force in April 1972, Marge and I moved to Ruston, Louisiana, so that I could enroll in Louisiana Tech in the fall. This time around, there would be no partying when I should be studying. Although I was blessed with a photographic memory, based on my previous academic performance, I wasn't entirely convinced that my second attempt at college would be the charm.

I had good reason to be uncertain. I had chosen medical technology as my major, simply because it didn't require a speech course. Who does that? Who heads down an entirely unknown road to avoid what isn't even certain to be a minor bump on another road? What a way to determine one's career path! It's ironic to think that I was once afraid of public speaking, but I suppose it just goes to show that God really does protect fools like me.

Maybe it was because I had Marge at my side this time around, but I made the decision to throw myself into my education with everything I had. It didn't take long to start seeing results. I made straight A's the first quarter. Much as I had done when working ten-hour days to buy that surfboard, I experienced the rewards of hard work. In fact, for my entire undergraduate program I earned straight A's, except for one B which I'm still sore about, because the professor just didn't like me and refused to give me the A I actually deserved. I even had a poem published in the school paper, though due to a mix-up it appeared in print under the wrong name!

I managed to extend the streak through graduate school. I decided to pursue an advanced degree after realizing that there wasn't much money to be made without one. I'd likely be stuck as a medical technologist, the lowest-paying position in the health care field. A Master of Science degree in clinical microbiology made sense, as it would complement my Bachelor of Science field of study. With it, I could someday—if everything went according to plan—earn considerably more money as a lab supervisor. Little did I know that the degree would become valuable for an entirely unexpected but very welcome reason.

Before I came to realize the true worth of my microbiology education, however, I discovered that clinical microbiology wasn't all that exciting and the money wasn't that much better either.

After I graduated with my Master's, I took a position at Highlands General Hospital in Shreveport, Louisiana. On my first day, the lab supervisor guided me into a lab that was so small you couldn't change your mind in it. Then he told me that not only was this microbiology lab going to be my office, but I was also going to be its supervisor. Essentially, I was going to be my own supervisor!

Although I enjoyed working in health science, the days I spent looking at slides of poop under a microscope were mind-numbingly uneventful. The lab was in the basement of the hospital, and I spent all day every day down there by myself, having very little interaction with other people. So, when salesmen stopped by, it was memorable—and not just for the human contact.

There was only one window in the lab, which looked out on the hospital's parking lot. The view outside was typically as uninspiring as the work I was doing inside. However, during those times when the salesmen visited, I was offered a glimpse of a life I didn't have…and it was a life I wanted. The salesmen drove fancy cars and wore well-cut suits. They wore Rolex watches and expensive shoes. And they seemed comfortable with their success and satisfied with their lives. I wasn't.

There was no logical reason for me to think, *if they can do it, I can too*. My instinct should probably have been to stay focused on working my way up the ladder one rung at a time. Instead, on those days when one of the salesmen stopped by, I would ask them if there was any way they could get me into a sales position. Their typical reply was "Sure, I'll help you out—just give me an order for my product first." I should probably have accepted that as a sign that I would be better off getting back to my poop slides, but I didn't. After multiple times asking but getting no useful answers, I realized that if the salesmen weren't going to help this lab rat find his way out of the lab—and they very obviously were not—the lab rat would have to find his own way out.

One of the hallmarks of a good salesman is to take "no" as a signal that the negotiation has only gotten started. Whatever the reason for my inability to accept their rejection, I was unfazed. I surged forward into the future I would shape myself.

I started out by grabbing the *Journal of Clinical Microbiology* and writing to every single company that advertised in its pages. I mailed out ninety-nine resumés. Over the next few weeks, I received ninety-eight responses thanking me for reaching out, saying that I had a great resumé, and assuring me I would be kept in mind for future positions. In short, my resumé ended up in the circular file—the trash can!

At my ninety-day review with my lab supervisor, he said what I should have been excited to hear: I was doing a great job. *Tell me something I don't know*, I thought instead.

I might have actually whispered it under my breath, because what my boss said was surely intended as either a threat or an incentive: "If you keep your nose to the grindstone, one day you will get my job."

As would happen throughout my life, I acted impulsively and said something I shouldn't have. It was something I had no right to be confident or stupid enough to verbalize. But I did it anyway. "I don't want your job."

"Why?" he asked, rightfully hostile.

The supervisor's office was bigger than mine, but it felt like the walls were closing in on me. I desperately performed the mental calculations to figure out what kind of money he was talking about me being able to make. At that time, I was making six dollars an hour. The lab supervisor's salary was $25,000 a year. That meant he was making more than double what I was making.

I thought again about that window through which I watched salesmen leave with their lucrative orders, and I said, "It doesn't pay enough."

Not for the last time in my life, I went home unsure of what to tell Marge about my day at work.

When I mailed my resumé out, unsolicited, to the companies I found in the *Journal of Clinical Microbiology*, I had for good measure also sent copies to some headhunters. At the time, Marge was six months pregnant. She had a doctor she trusted and a husband who was, after years of sacrifice in pursuit of it, in a stable microbiology job he loved … or so she thought.

The day after it became clear to my supervisor and me that I didn't have a future at Highlands General Hospital, I received a call from one of the headhunters. I may have been less than strategic when I sent out my resumé in scattershot fashion a few weeks before, but it turned out I was in fact qualified for a sales position. My lab days would be behind me. I would finally be doing sales!

Without consulting my heavily pregnant wife, I accepted the job.

Unfortunately, the poultry business wasn't all that much more exciting than medical lab work. This was a realization I didn't come to until after Marge and I had relocated to Eldorado, Arkansas, where I went to work for JM Poultry.

My time in the chicken business did, however, teach me an important lesson. I think most people are at least vaguely aware that in order for a chick to emerge from an egg, it must first break though the shell. Chicks will peck and peck and finally, after significant time and effort, break free. It can be pretty uncomfortable watching those little birds work so hard. Human instinct may cause us to want to help them get an easier start, but there is a good reason for all that work. When chicks don't hatch as nature intended, their neck muscles don't become strong enough to support their heads. Ultimately, they are unable to survive.

Perhaps my stint in "chicken world" should be viewed the same way—as a mistake that I had to make in order to live a better life.

While working in the chicken processing plant—which was something I had to do in order to learn the business before being promoted into sales or management—I received an unexpected call from a man named Jim Digh. Jim said he was with a company called

Analytab Products, and they were looking for a microbiologist who could sell their products.

Although I didn't know it at the time, Analytab's interest in hiring a microbiologist to do sales represented leading-edge business thinking. Typically, trained salespeople were taught the science behind the products. But because Analytab's products were so technical, Jim believed that microbiologists could be trained to sell.

Jim may have suspected that I was the right person for the job, but I certainly didn't. I was in Arkansas, in the chicken business—it was clear that I had no idea who I was or what I should be doing.

The name of the company didn't ring a bell at first. Since I was finally about to start management training at JM Poultry after my purgatory in the processing plant, I thanked Jim for his interest but told him that I was already in a sales position. It was only when Jim mentioned having my resumé sitting in front of him that I made the connection: Analytab Products was number ninety-nine on the list of companies to which I had sent my resumé while working in the hospital basement lab. Despite Jim's obvious belief that the position at Analytab would be a good fit for me, I was unable to predict the strain that accepting such a job would put on my marriage. So I declined to be interviewed.

Three months later, at the conclusion of my JM Poultry sales training program, I was in my boss's office to discuss the next steps in my career.

"We're sending you out to Colorado," my boss said, "to one of our cold-storage facilities."

I imagine that the expression on my face must have been much like the one I'd shown my lab supervisor at Highlands General

Hospital. "I have a master's degree in clinical microbiology. I don't want to work in a cold-storage plant!"

I went to talk to Marge, who was in her hospital bed with our newborn son in her arms. I hadn't been in the room long before asking what she thought about me leaving JM Poultry. She responded, "I don't think now is a good time." Her response, as usual, wasn't what I had hoped for. It was, as usual, what I deserved.

I didn't want to upset Marge, yet I hoped that she might reconsider. So I asked again, "What would you think if I left my job?"

"Chuck," she said while tending to Seth, who was starting to fuss, "I *really* don't think now is a good time."

Marge was right. It wasn't a good time to give up my position. But I'd already done it. I had quit JM Poultry earlier that very day.

* * *

I have trouble pinpointing what made it so much more difficult many years later to do the same thing, when I had to go home and tell Marge about what had happened at EnviroMed (another of my pre-Vanguard business ventures). Maybe it was because by that time we had four children instead of two. Or because after years of moving across the country—nineteen moves in thirteen years, and every child born in a different state—Marge thought EnviroMed would provide our family with the means to settle down and appreciate the fruits of our labor.

Marge had astutely recognized early in our marriage that family life would be impossible for us if we were chasing competing career opportunities, so we had made the decision that she would run the home and raise the children. She worked harder than I ever did and was forced to sacrifice more for my career than I ever had.

So, I didn't fear her reaction or pity myself for what had been done to me at EnviroMed. Plain and simple, I didn't want to tell her because Marge didn't deserve to have her husband come home yet again and announce that the life she so clearly deserved was, once again, over.

CHAPTER 5

FANTASY LAND

Fate is not the ruler, but the servant of providence.
— Edward G. Bulwer-Lytton

No matter what may happen during my workday—and there have been some *very* eventful days over the course of my career—I have always relished coming home to Marge. She is my foundation, my touchstone. No other woman could have survived what she did or put up with as much as she was forced to.

Marge credits the independence and self-reliance she gained in her childhood for her ability to cope with the challenges that came against us. She is just an exceptional person. The faith we found during our college years taught her how to endure hardships with grace and fortifies her against anything she has to go through. She rests in the confidence that this earth isn't her true home, and that any challenges she experiences now are only temporary.

I've always been driven to succeed. Always someone who considered himself a millionaire just waiting until he can cash the check. Despite her acceptance and apparent ease in acclimating to any situation, Marge has sometimes paid a high price for my ambition.

On the Friday evening after matters at EnviroMed came to a head, I drove home, but didn't immediately go inside the house. I just couldn't face Marge. Whether through my own fault or circumstances beyond my control, our family was again now in financial jeopardy. I typically walked straight into a home filled with noise and children and pets. That was the family we had both always yearned for, so we had created it for ourselves. On that day, however, I remained in my car, my fingers loosely gripping the keys that were still hanging from the ignition. When I eventually mustered up the courage to turn off the engine, I had reached the point where I needed Marge more than I feared the dread that had roared to life within me.

Sitting in my car, I watched movement stirring behind the windows of the house. My family had always trusted me to provide, to keep them safe and secure. Now, my perspective of being on the outside looking in revealed to me all the ways I had been absent. I had been forging a career that I believed Marge and our children would benefit from, but they had been the ones sacrificing for it.

How could I possibly go into the house and tell Marge what had happened?

When I finally mustered the strength to tell her, she understood and, as always, supported me fully. "EnviroMess," is what she calls it today. Not back then, while we were in the middle of it, of course. If we had admitted to each other then, or even to ourselves during quiet moments of contemplation, the extent of the emotional and financial mess we were in, I don't know if we would have been able to get out of it and move forward. Not as a couple, anyway.

* * *

After my premature departure from chicken world, I had swallowed my pride and called up my mother to ask if we could temporarily stay with them in Fort Myers while I looked for a new job. (Make no mistake: neither Marge nor I were looking forward to living with my parents any longer than was absolutely necessary.)

As expected, my mother didn't make it easy for me. "How are you planning to support your family?"

"God will provide," I said.

With her typical dry wit, my mother responded, "Please don't confuse God with your father."

We had no choice. We moved our family back to Florida. I thought about Jim Digh and how he'd said he needed a microbiologist to sell for Analytab Products. No longer having a job to lose, I decided to call Jim up and tell him that I was available for the position, if it was still open.

"Chicken business not going well, Chuck?" he said, letting out a boisterous laugh.

We joked a bit about my stint at JM Poultry. In fact, we would laugh about it together for some time to come; so, Jim hired me for the position I had initially turned down.

Analytab brought me on sixty days ahead of the next sales training session. Jim and I didn't do much additional talking before I started. He did, however, fly down to Florida for what I naively expected would be intensive one-on-one sales lessons. What I got instead were two things I needed, both hurriedly delivered. First was a reminder that God gave us two ears and one mouth for a reason— if I listened twice as much as I talked, clients *would* tell me what they needed. Second, he handed me a book containing the names and contact information of current and prospective clients.

As he turned to leave, he paused and shared what I imagine he considered sage wisdom. "Do you know the story of Samson and the Philistines?" he asked. When I confirmed that I did, he hit me with it: "Then you know he killed three thousand of those dudes with the jawbone of an ass. Remember that every day, many sales are killed with the same weapon." Then he winked, smiled, and was gone, leaving me with little more than my obvious ignorance and an obstinate determination to be a great salesman.

I confess to not following protocol. But how was I even to *know* the protocol? I didn't worry about simply picking up the phone and going right to the top, unintentionally (though fortuitously) bypassing the people who *should* have been placing the orders with me. Not knowing what I didn't know, I threw myself into the job and worked a ten-hour day every day. Thankfully, from the exponential increase in orders coming in as I built my base, it was clear that I had found my mojo. I hadn't known for certain that I would have what it took.

Within six months, not only was I the top salesman in the region—the region being the entire state of Florida—but I was the top salesman in *all* the regions. I relied on my hard-learned lessons from managing my father's trauma and some offhand advice from other salespeople. With that foundation, I had become Analytab Products' number-one salesman in the nation. I was covering a large territory, and our townhouse's location just north of Miami wasn't going to work for us much longer. So off we went to Orlando, where we purchased a trilevel home on a cul-de-sac that offered me easier travel access. One of the unintended consequences of my stellar sales performance was that my overnight travel increased to the point that I was away from home Monday through Friday, and only around on the weekends.

Maybe Marge's love for the new house made my absence easier on her and the kids. But, as was becoming a pattern for me, I was getting comfortable enough to feel a familiar itch. My restlessness bordered on agitation. Marge and I knew this would soon be followed by angst if I didn't take some action.

I put out a few feelers to see if there was a better paying sales position available anywhere else. It didn't take long for a headhunter to find me something. Baxter Travenol was a large company that sold IV solutions to hospitals. If I got the job, my income would jump by 20 percent and I would only have to be away from home two nights a week. *If* I got the job. First, I had to beat out thirty-nine other applicants to get it.

I was selected for an interview, and felt that the conversation with Dick Charland, the Travenol district manager, went well. However, as we were wrapping up the interview, my mind jumped to consider those thirty-nine other applicants. As I had already done a few times by this point in my career, I blurted out something unplanned and, in all likelihood, completely unreasonable. "If you don't hire me, you'll be making a mistake!"

I discovered after the fact that Dick had already settled on hiring another candidate *before* he interviewed me. He had all but made the offer. Then I fired my parting shot. That night, as Dick tells it, he couldn't stop thinking about what I'd said to him. And he changed his mind, offering me the job the next morning.

I can't take any credit for being right, but it turned out that I was. Another position at Travenol became available in Jacksonville shortly after I was hired. It made sense for Dick to offer this role to the candidate he'd originally intended to hire for my position. The new hire lasted only two months.

The Travenol position worked well for Marge and me. The irony that I had initially chosen a career in medical technology because I was afraid of public speaking, yet ended up being a salesman who thrived on face-to-face interaction, wasn't lost on either of us. To this day, I believe that the reason I flourished was because of the practice I'd had as a boy at managing my dad's unpredictable war-related outbursts. As has been said, "All things work together for good." Marge and I were beginning to recognize that something greater—call it fate or, as she and I do, providence—had a hand in our lives.

The GI Bill ensured that my undergraduate and graduate degrees had set us back only $1,200. Though the first few years of our married life were still a struggle, now, for the first time as a couple, we had some extra income. Our investment in my career, from college to the many relocations we had undertaken, was finally paying dividends. The wind was decidedly at our backs.

Travenol relocated us again, this time to Gainesville, Florida. As always, Marge was everything a husband could hope for. I often told our children how lucky they were to have her as their mother—and how I wished I'd had a mother like her. I quickly advanced to become the top salesman in the district, and was working toward becoming number one in the region. This meant long days for me and not enough time with my family.

Even though my presence in the children's lives was more limited than I would have liked for it to have been, it still had an impact. As I reflect now, although Joanne and Nathan, our two youngest children, hadn't been born when I started at Travenol, the influence of this time in my career would be easily discerned in all of my children's skill sets and career choices.

That influence can be seen in the events of one particular evening some years later. I was sitting on the couch when my younger daughter, Joanne, went running past me carrying an armful of Ziploc bags.

"What are you doing?" I asked her.

"Bringing them to Nathan," she called over her shoulder.

"What does Nathan need Ziploc bags for?"

"For the candy he's selling at school."

I called Nathan out from his bedroom to the couch. "What's going on?"

"Well," he said, "Mom buys Airheads at Sam's for five cents apiece. I bag them and sell them for a quarter each, or five for a dollar."

Warmed by my twelve-year-old son's business savvy, I asked, "How many are you selling?"

"About twenty a day," he said, shrugging. "Twenty bucks a week."

The next afternoon, I got a call from the school, saying that Nathan was stealing the other kids' lunch money. I explained what was going on—that the kids were using their lunch money to buy the candy. I was told this practice had to stop. It nearly broke my heart to do it, but I was forced to share with Nathan that his days as a schoolyard salesman were over.

* * *

It now seems like a lifetime ago that I sat in Alachua General Hospital in Gainesville, next to that salesman who was sloppily dressed. When he told me was an independent sales rep, I had no idea what that was. Then he told me about the $125,000 a year he was making and, just like that, the old restlessness was back.

"I'm going to be an independent sales rep," I told Marge later that night, lying in bed after the kids had gone to sleep.

"What is that?" she asked.

"I don't know," I responded, "but they make a lot of money."

Not long after, I met Clay and Jeff at a trade show. They told me they were starting a new company called Sterile Design and were in need of independent sales reps. Just like that, I went home and announced to Marge that, after only one year in Gainesville, we were moving to Durham, North Carolina.

New job. New house. New territory. What could possibly go wrong?

A lot, as it turned out. The snowstorm in Burlington on my first day of sales calls was, I now recognize, an omen. Perhaps if I had heeded that omen, I could have avoided some of the struggles we faced over the following year.

I'll never forget the materials manager who didn't show up for our scheduled appointment. It was only after I had loudly voiced my displeasure that his secretary told me the that he had died!

Then there was the attitude embodied in a portly old purchasing agent who sat smoking a fat cigar in his hospital office. Although he seemed to listen intently as I made my pitch for custom procedure trays, he leaned back in his chair and looked up as if studying the ceiling for a long moment. Finally, he released a puff of smoke and responded, "Custom trays, huh? I'll tell ya what, young man. If I ever have the need for custom procedure trays, I'll give you a call."

Compounding my sales challenges was the fact that we had a measly seven hundred dollars in our bank account. This paltry amount meant we were "too rich" to have our application for government assistance approved. We explained that the money would be gone as soon as we paid the next month's rent. We were told, "Then come back next month."

I applied to the hospital's finance department for a grant under the Hill-Burton Act, which provided for free or reduced-cost health care, to help cover the cost of the birth of Joanne, our third child. At the same time, I was trying to sell custom procedure trays to the hospital's operating room and hoping that no one in finance found out.

Next came a blown-out transmission, which literally fell out of our Chevy Nova while we were driving home from the hospital in the middle of winter with newborn Joanne.

My first sale in Durham was, at the time, the biggest order in Sterile Design's history, but nevertheless Marge and I found ourselves perennially short of money. It wasn't that I wasn't making sales, because I was. I just couldn't ramp up those sales fast enough to bring in sufficient commissions to cover our costs. As a result, we spent that first year treading water. That is, until Bill Frisbey recognized that a wave was about to take us under.

Bill had been my first trainer back at Travenol. I was a good salesman; Bill was a great one. He was informed, well-spoken, and highly personable. Bill and I had been together in the IV Solutions division, but then I'd left Gainesville for Durham while Bill stayed in Orlando. We'd lost track of each other while I was up in North Carolina, and during that time Bill had hooked up with Clay Page. Their partnership admittedly had left me feeling somewhat out in the cold.

As circumstances had changed, Bill now offered me a low draw against commission to move down to Lakeland and sell for

Custom Medical Products, the exclusive distributor in Florida for Sterile Design. My old trainer was also willing to give me the potentially very profitable Tampa Bay territory.

So back to Florida Marge and I went. I was still working long days, but unlike in North Carolina, one of my very first sales calls paid off.

I was sitting in the radiology department at University Community Hospital in Tampa, Florida, waiting to see the chief tech about a custom radiology tray. Alongside me in the waiting room were patients and their families, and seated next to me was an older lady. In truth, I was so focused on reviewing my presentation that I didn't realize she had noticed my briefcase and was looking intently at me. "Are you a salesman?" she asked.

I wanted to be nice to this woman, who appeared to be in her mid-sixties, but I also needed to concentrate. I gave her a quick smile and a hasty yes, then got back to my business.

"My husband was a salesman," she interrupted me again, "and a very good one at that!"

It was clear that I wasn't going to get any work done, so I stopped reading.

"You do know, don't you, that when a salesman asks for the order, the first one to speak loses?" she said.

She had my attention. "Does that really work?" I asked incredulously.

Nodding, she said, "My husband swore by it."

Moments later, I was called into the chief tech's office. I went over the custom tray and its cost as I typically would, and asked him to give me a purchase order. Then I closed my mouth and I waited.

It seemed like an eternity. *Tick, tick, tick* went the hands of an unseen clock on the wall behind me. Although I didn't move a muscle, my brain was scrambling with the question of when this torture would end.

Then he said, quite simply, "Sure."

Son of a biscuit, she was right, I thought. I exhaled and felt the pressure that had built during the longest five seconds of my life turn to relief.

Thanks to the angel in the University Community Hospital waiting room, this was the turning point in my sales ability. To this day, I rely on the technique she gifted me.

Bill may have recognized that there was potential in the Tampa Bay territory, but I give all credit for my success to this technique. My sales went off like a series of well-timed explosions, paying off at the right times. Marge and I had all the reason in the world to believe that this was *our time* and that nothing could stop us.

Even Dick Isel, who provoked a blowup unlike any I had experienced before or since, did little more than slow us down temporarily. I left Sterile Design and went to work for DeRoyal, a company that, despite being Sterile Design's biggest competitor, didn't know one thing about getting costs down on custom trays. They were only too happy to learn from me.

I sued Sterile Design for the $20,000 in moving expenses I hadn't been paid. Dick wasn't willing to go down without a fight, though, and Sterile Design countersued me for violation of the noncompete in my employment agreement. What followed was too much litigation that went on for too long under the direction of my not-especially-bright attorney. We ended up settling for $17,000, and I called it a draw.

It was 1984, and I was eager to put Sterile Design in my rearview mirror. But that couldn't happen until the company was sold to Johnson & Johnson. Thanks to the stock I had purchased when I was first hired by Sterile Design, I ended up making some money. I also got my first taste of the power and wealth company stock could provide. I became an entrepreneur, and I never worked for another company.

I left DeRoyal in 1985, right around the time they were marketing a reusable surgical towel as single-use. I couldn't have imagined how such an arbitrary classification, made by the companies who profited from the product in question, would take hold of my life. As I saw it at the time, I was just "doing my towels."

Staying true to my desire to work for myself, I started a company called Diversified Medical Incorporated (DiMed). Many area hospitals had already made the switch to disposable surgical towels, gowns, and drapes, as this was right around the time an active push to protect the environment had begun to take hold. My idea was to start a company that would focus on recycling reusable surgical towels, gowns, and drapes, thereby saving the hospitals money and reducing the volume of medical waste that was going into our landfills.

The strategy consisted of collecting the surgical towels from DeRoyal's nationwide hospital accounts—the towels labeled "single-use"—and reprocessing them by washing, drying, and sterilizing them. I would then resell these towels to the hospitals. After about a year of running the business from our home on Bruton Road, which was providentially zoned for agriculture, I brought Tom Howard on board, believing his experience as a founder at Sterile Design would be of great benefit to someone like me, who was looking to do something new in the industry. How wrong I turned out to be.

To increase our business, we knew we needed to augment the number of towels we were collecting from the hospitals. After some digging, we discovered that we could buy cheap towels from China, so we did. The problem was that in those days, the American government placed quotas on Chinese imports, and we weren't able to buy as many towels as we needed. It was a setback that forced us to get more sophisticated.

Tom and I decided to leverage the existing environmental interest and changed the company's name from DiMed to EnviroMed. Next, we needed to raise equity. We sought and received approximately two million dollars in equity from two venture capitalists. I drew on a friend's existing relationship with an associate in Haiti to secure low cost of production. Compared to costs in the Far East, Haiti looked like the right place for us to produce our own towels.

After returning from a trip to Haiti to tour the facilities, Tom and I located a shut-down textile producer, Dakota Mills, in North Carolina. We bought all of their looms and dyeing equipment, with the idea that we would ship the gear to Haiti, where the actual weaving of the towels would happen.

If I were to pinpoint what aspect of EnviroMed was responsible for my demise, it would have to be assigning Tom the task of getting the equipment installed and the towels produced. The agreed-on budget was one million dollars. But without my knowledge, and without an alert to the board of directors, Tom spent almost two million—all of the company's cash—while I was out trying to line up sales.

That decision put EnviroMed on the verge of collapse, and me on the verge of committing homicide. Tom and I met with the board and explained what had happened. Surprisingly, they went easy on us and agreed without any protestation to put up additional money. Injecting more cash meant that they collectively became the major shareholders, in the position to make decisions for the company. They wanted to make just one.

They determined that the company would issue stock for pennies on the dollar. I was adamantly opposed to this, and naturally assumed my partner's thinking would be in alignment. Looking back, it's crystal clear how far off base I was with this line of thinking. Although I had *believed* that Tom had given me advance warning of his ineptitude, he had in fact *already* informed the board, and a joint strategy between Tom and the board had been prepared before I learned of Tom's overspending. I walked right into a setup.

It turned out I hadn't given Tom the credit he deserved for his business acumen. He voted with the board, and I was fired.

* * *

How could I possibly tell Marge what had happened, when at the time I barely understood it myself? We'd started our life together with nothing more than a few hundred dollars and a low-paying job. Now we were $250,000 in debt—and there was no job.

At forty years old, with four children ranging in age from eight to sixteen, I had to go into the house that I feared we were about to lose and explain why.

As it turned out, I wasn't telling Marge anything she didn't already know. A few weeks before, as she did from time to time, she had visited me at the EnviroMed office. She didn't stop by because she found it hard to separate herself from the business. She was only too pleased to have the company operating out of a separate space and not from inside her home, as it had when it was still DiMed. Though she was concerned about the vast amount of space Tom and I had leased, it sure beat having workers in her kitchen.

Marge wasn't looking for anything in particular on her visit and had no reason to be suspicious. She had no cause to think there was anything amiss with the business. But the contrast she observed between my desk and Tom's made it abundantly clear that something was very much amiss.

At home or at work, I don't like a lot of clutter. Marge loves her knick-knacks, appreciating the deals she gets almost as much as the items themselves. The running joke is that if the government were to come into our house and confiscate everything that cost more than twenty-five dollars, we would keep almost every single item. When it comes to my personal working space, though, I prefer to have around me only the items I use.

So, when Marge saw the state of my typically utilitarian desktop, she was immediately puzzled. Stacks of paper. Open folders. Binders in piles. No desktop to be seen. Not only was my desk a cluttered mess, but I didn't even seem to be aware of it. I barely had time to lift my head and greet her.

Tom's desk was a very different story. Marge found it to be, as usual, an expanse of smooth, uninterrupted glass top. Tom's back was to the doorway, where she stood unnoticed. As she waited for him to sense her presence, she noticed that he was clicking away at what she recognized was the EnviroMed revenue forecast. Marge knew a thing or two about how a company's finances work, having grown up watching her father do the books for the family business. Seeing the sales projections—where the company needed to get to, and how overwhelmed I was trying to get it there alone—she had just one thought: *This isn't going to last.*

Marge removed the three Bible verses that we'd displayed on the wall. She thought that in their place—or, even better, hanging above Tom's office door—should be a sign that read FANTASY LAND. When she walked back into my office, she held the framed verses under her arm. Closing the door, she asked, "Who is in control here?" She placed the cherished verses on the chair she was too anxious to sit in.

"What do you mean?" I asked, my nose still buried in something or other. Near my elbow were the marketing materials that Tom had, without consulting me, decided to cut me out of. Instead of us appearing together as partners, Tom and a nice lady who was doing some work for the company, a former Tampa Bay Buccaneers cheerleader, were advertised as the faces of EnviroMed. The slick new marketing was telling a story that Tom wasn't telling me.

"This is not good, Chuck," Marge said. "Whoever signs the checks is in control, and you are no longer signing the checks."

I knew she was right; of course I did. But what choice did I have? As long as I was still trying, there was still hope.

From the expression on Marge's face, she wasn't convinced that I was taking her warning seriously. What she didn't know was that I had also seen Tom's desk. I recognized that, while I was becoming ever more overwhelmed, nothing on his side had changed.

The last thing my wife said before picking up the framed verses and leaving was, "I'm going to take these before everything falls apart."

So as I stood facing Marge in the living room, with what felt like everything fallen all around us, exhaustion writ across my face and defeat in my posture, there was nothing she could have said—nothing I could ever have wanted her to say—that would mean more than "Chuck, you were fighting a battle you couldn't win."

Marge knew how hard I had worked. More importantly, she knew that what had happened wasn't my fault. So, with Marge's arms around me, I found myself at home in a way that no one could ever take from us.

Part II

A Call to Arms

There is a time to take counsel of your fears, and there is a time to never listen to any fear.

— George S. Patton

CHAPTER 6

CIRCLE THE WAGONS

The most important lesson to remember is that failure is inevitable, but so is success, so rebound.

— Naveen Tewari

It was Monday morning, the first Monday after I was fired from EnviroMed. The start of the work week—and the first time in my professional life that I had absolutely nowhere to be. It had only been three days, and I was already lost in the sense of stagnation that had burrowed deep into my soul.

The weekend passed in a blur as I did little more than sit on the couch while the household continued to function noisily around me. But the internal silence was deafening. My memory tells me that I sat on that couch for that entire Monday, marking the longest period of time in my adult life that I have remained entirely still. The stillness wasn't serenity or stoicism. It was shock—staggering, stupefying, soul-draining shock.

As Nathan, our youngest child, tells it today, I wasn't actually still. In fact, I was anything *but* still. Instead of stewing on the couch, he recalls me stalking the house like a caged animal, pacing back and forth as I raged. None of the children could understand my being at the house during the day, and they didn't know what to make of it. Mostly the kids knew they should just steer clear of me.

Maybe the silence I recall wasn't imagined, and perhaps the children were intentionally keeping quiet and out of my way to ensure that I didn't lash out at them. My being suddenly at home was not easy on Marge either.

From the time my brother Ted and I had become adults and started to talk openly about our upbringing, he (with the benefit of six years of therapy) and I have readily agreed that he is more like our well-intentioned father, while I have the tendency to stir the pot, much as my mother did. It's something that I have to guard myself against, even to this day. Marge and the kids had established a daily routine that was heavily dependent on my work, my goals, my schedule, and my travel itinerary—and it functioned better without input from me.

As our oldest son, Seth, vividly recalls, he only became aware that something had gone wrong with my job when I arrived home from work the Friday evening of my firing. Marge and I had already agreed that Seth could sleep over at his best friend's house that night, but when I walked in the door, it was clear that this was no longer going to happen. The reason? Seth's best friend was also the son of my now-former partner, Tom Howard.

When it came to Marge's response to my presence in the house, all I can say is that I recognize just how fortunate I was that she focused all of her impressive ire on Tom, and not on me.

One of those first nights after Tom's betrayal, Marge and I were lying awake in bed because neither of us could fall asleep. I was turning over in my mind how I could get us out of this mess and get us back on our feet as quickly as possible. Meanwhile, my wife, the sweetest woman you could ever meet, was thinking up ways that

Tom might be knocked off *his* feet. Nothing too malevolent, of course, but a particularly uncomfortable case of stomach flu or an unpleasant encounter with a beehive sounded about right.

Whether because I failed to predict what Tom was capable of or, allowed him to come in as a true fifty-percent partner, I was ultimately responsible for EnviroMess, but that didn't matter to Marge. I never experienced from her, even for one minute, the sense that I had failed or wronged our family.

Instead of turning against me, Marge turned toward me, and together we started to make plans. Marge's toughness, resourcefulness, and unyielding faith in me were all brought to bear as she laid the groundwork for how we would survive this setback, emotionally, mentally, financially, and otherwise.

In that moment, lying in darkness and sensing the light of her spirit, I felt she gave me more than I could have ever imagined— certainly more than any man could deserve. I tell people, "If you call me an asshole in front of Marge, you may be right … but you will only gain a lifelong enemy."

It quickly became apparent that the friends who had been at my side on the way up weren't necessarily going to remain at my side during the fall—not that I could blame them. After the initial shock wore off, I was plunged into a period of deep reflection, some might even call it depression, during which I was forced to examine my attitudes and actions from the preceding years. I had time to think about how I treated people, how I made them feel, what motivated me, and what mattered to me.

It is said that pride goes before a fall. Had I been too proud? Did I somehow deserve this? I knew with certainty that Marge and the children did not. The thought of them having to endure uncertainty over how we would survive sank me lower than I could ever have imagined. As parents, we had always tried to shield our children from the challenges of our family finances. The thought of any of them worrying and suffering as a result of what had happened with EnviroMed was unbearable for me. Marge and I had never come this close to not being able to cover the essentials. We were in real trouble and I had to do *something*.

Although I didn't feel any positivity about my circumstances, I knew I had to put a positive spin on things—possibly for myself, but certainly for others. People instinctively respond to positivity; they seek it out. And people guard themselves against self-pitying behaviors. This was a time in my life when I needed others to feel comfortable being around me. Wallowing and complaining wasn't going to endear me to anyone. I had never needed my people skills—or people who might connect me to the next opportunity—more than now.

At the same time, I wasn't going to hide what had happened to me. I ran into someone I knew who said, "How've you been, Chuck? I heard you got screwed."

I told them, "Marge and I hit a bump in the road, no doubt about that, but we're looking forward to the future and have every reason to be optimistic about it."

That was the end of it—the last mention of EnviroMed in our conversation. I didn't vent every time I was given the chance or take every opportunity to share my tale of woe. I said that I was grateful for the experience and was using it as an opportunity. I don't know if I initially believed what I was telling people, or how long it took for me to believe it, but I made sure to act like I did.

Marge has an apt metaphor to describe me. She says I'm like a buoy out on the ocean. No matter how violent the waves or how long I'm held under the water, I will bounce back up to the top, as resilient as ever. No matter how I'm pressed down, I can't help but rise to the surface.

Marge worked the numbers to budget our meager resources while I took stock of my skills. I sat on the couch and thought long and hard about myself. Let me tell you, examining yourself in such a way after you've spent so long defining yourself in terms of hours worked, deals closed, and job titles achieved, is no easy task. I'd been working since I was a teenager, but where did my talents actually lie? What was I good at and enjoyed doing?

The answer to every question I asked was *sales*. It was what filled me with confidence, excited me, and would allow me to best support my family, what would challenge and engage me. I had spent the past fifteen years honing the skills I relied on in childhood to diffuse those dangerous situations with my father and I had become a successful salesman, thanks in part to him. I also loved *being* a salesman. Selling to people was not only a productive exchange but an enjoyable one—for them and for me.

I needed to get back to selling.

Thankfully, I discovered that there was still a need for my particular set of skills. Even as I was questioning so much about who I believed I was, I didn't doubt that I had to keep my promise to myself to stay independent. I needed to maintain some sense of control at a time when I felt unmoored.

The initial step I took was to incorporate as a consulting business under the name Vanguard Medical Concepts. My first customer was Charleston Area Medical Center (CAMC), which offered me a short-term consulting contract. I spent several months in West Virginia and supported the family from there.

CAMC, one of the largest employers in the state of West Virginia, paid me fifty thousand dollars to help them better understand costs and whether they should make the move to produce their own custom procedure trays. Although CAMC ultimately decided to stay with their current vendor, thanks to my help, they were able to get a much better deal. I felt pretty good about that—especially since their vendor was DeRoyal! At the time, I had no way of knowing just how vindictive manufacturers can be, and how personally they take it when you mess with their bottom line.

My next move was to attend the 1991 Association of Operating Room Nurses (AORN) Surgical Conference and Expo, the largest gathering of perioperative nurses in the nation, which was being held that year in Atlanta, Georgia. My plan was to hunt for manufacturers who were looking for independent sales reps to carry their products, and I found them.

Don Burt, who had introduced Tom Howard and me to EnviroMed's production contact in Haiti, was also in the medical devices field. Don happened to have a vendor's booth at AORN that year. He knew of my situation and was kind enough to let me make the drive with him from Tampa to Atlanta. He even allowed me to share his hotel room.

At the conference, I furtively ate my dinners in the manufacturers' hospitality suites, which offered big buffet tables of hors d'oeuvres. I was in a sorry situation, hungry and unable to buy myself dinner.

Also attending the conference was Dick Isel—a man about whom it was once said, "Wherever Dick goes, he makes money while others lose it." I don't know which was worse: avoiding Dick or sneaking into those hospitality suites for dinner.

I would gladly have eaten my lunches there too, except lunches weren't catered. So, on my first afternoon, I left the conference center and walked over to a McDonalds. Back then you could buy two burgers for a dollar. I lowered myself into a plastic chair and unwrapped my sad-looking burgers. As I bit into the first bun, I felt hot tears streaming down my face. *How did I get here? Just how the hell did I get here?*

Sitting in that fast-food joint was an emotional and spiritual turning point for me. I'm not sure of the source, but within a moment of roughly brushing away my tears, I heard, *"Stop it, you're fine."* The *"you're fine"* echoed from somewhere deep within me. And yes, I was. I was alive. I was fine. I would move on, and soon I would be better than fine.

I stopped crying and closed the door on any emotion I felt about my situation. Finishing the burgers, I rose from my seat and returned to a conference where thousands of decision-makers were just waiting for me. They would play a role—a supporting role—in my rise from an almighty fall.

By the time I returned to Florida, I was carrying a few products and calling on hospitals in the Tampa Bay area, starting over in the same territory I had once dominated. Although humbling, it was an opportunity I was grateful to have. It was an opportunity I was hell-bent on seizing.

CHAPTER 7

WHAT'S IN A LABEL?

Perception is reality.

— Lee Atwater

In industry jargon, an SUD is the term coined by the FDA to describe a single-use device. There are inarguable economic and environmental benefits to reprocessing SUDs. Nevertheless, in my heart of hearts, I don't believe anyone could have predicted the billion-dollar industry that would exist just twenty years after the founding of Vanguard.

It was Marge who recommended that we call the company Vanguard Medical Concepts. Our intent was for the name to represent the consulting I was doing at the time and would continue to do, staying true to my desire to work for myself. As it turned out, the people who joined me as employees and went on to become lifelong friends truly led a revolution in the SUD reprocessing industry.

Together, we embodied the definition of the word *vanguard*: being at the forefront of an action or movement. In our goal to make SUD reprocessing a legitimate, accepted practice, one without any stigma, we formed the leading edge. Vanguard was at the forefront of the fledgling SUD reprocessing industry. If you were to ask any former employee for their opinion of what we as a company did for the industry, they would be likely to say, *"I don't know how we did it, but we couldn't have done it with any other group of people or at any other time in health care."* I confidently second this assessment, but I remain astonished at all the things that had to happen that I didn't know had to happen, and, if they didn't happen would have put us out of business.

Medical devices aren't sexy, or flashy or exciting. Yet, when you or a family member is facing a surgical procedure, medical devices—pacemakers, infusion pumps, and even tongue depressors—can play a critical role in the outcome. The diagnostic, treatment, and quality-of-life implications of these devices can be profound. US health care costs reached $3.5 trillion dollars in 2017 alone. Medical device sales hit $172 billion in 2013 and have risen every year since. Make no mistake: the medical device industry is very profitable, and when profit is at risk, the stakes are high.

A defibrillator can save a life. That same defibrillator, when not safely designed, developed, or deployed, can also end a life. In order for a medical device to be deemed safe and effective, testing is necessary. Not surprisingly, the greater the associated risk, the more testing is needed.

Medical devices are classified according to their intended use and the type of contact they have with patients. Categories include critical or high-risk (balloon angioplasty catheters, implanted infusion pumps, and electrode recording catheters), semi-critical or medium-risk (orthopedic devices, ultrasound catheters, and laparoscopic equipment), and noncritical or low-risk (elastic bandaged, tourniquet cuffs, and blood-pressure cuffs). In recent years, technological advances have revolutionized many state-of-the-art devices, but *any* medical device is capable of negatively impacting a patient's care, and therefore must be held to the highest standard.

When it comes to the notion of *reprocessing* medical devices labeled for single use, defined by the Food and Drug Administration (FDA) as "intended for one use on a single patient during a single procedure." A reprocessed SUD is a device that has been previously used on a patient and has been subjected to additional processing for the purpose of enabling another single use on a patient. Therefore, the initial perception of health care providers was not good. They used words like: *Dirty. Unsafe. Ethically questionable. Dangerous.*

Reprocessing, whether of a reusable device or an SUD, is a process that includes the disinfection, cleaning, testing, packaging, labeling, and sterilization of a used medical device. Reprocessing any SUD has to meet requirements for cleanliness, function, and sterility. Even so, when it comes to reusing, for example, a scalpel, reactions can range from a visceral *yuck* to the emotional perception that the item must somehow be unsafe or ineffective.

Reprocessed SUDs would eventually be proven to have a defect rate five times lower than brand-new devices, yet our suggestion that saving money and protecting patients were not mutually exclusive was widely considered misguided or even deceptive. I always said that emotion was our biggest foe, while science was our closest friend.

Even when there was no immediate knee-jerk reaction, the perceptions of risk caused hesitation and outright stonewalling among hospitals, which were necessarily conscious of liability and patient safety. Three out of four surgeons believed that reprocessed SUDs posed a threat to their patients. Nearly as many nurses found the idea of a reprocessed SUD being used on them or a family member "uncomfortable." The wind was blowing against us, for these were our potential customers.

Detractors claimed that SUDs were safe and effective for a single use as annotated on the label, but that after that single use, the devices must surely become garbage. It never made sense to me that anyone would buy this argument, as no manufacturer concerned with safety and effectiveness would intentionally design and develop a device to stop functioning at 1.1 uses!

Prior to the Medicare Act of 1965, nearly every medical device was sold as reusable. Devices back then were largely made from glass, rubber, and metal, and were therefore only in need of hand wiping, dipping, and soaking in a disinfectant and/or sterilization before reuse. Thanks to the ease of cleaning and sterilizing such devices, in-house reprocessing in hospitals' central processing departments was considered safe.

But with advances in plastic technology, medical devices became smaller, more flexible, and more intricate. When Medicare started to reimburse based on cost, and original equipment manufacturers (OEMs) like Johnson & Johnson and Medtronic became aware of this policy, they labeled their products differently. In so doing, the OEMs became what I call the Big Dogs, who would protect their kingdom they'd claimed for themselves at all costs.

Medical device manufacturers were required to conduct stringent testing for reusable medical devices, and meeting FDA requirements meant that such devices could in fact be cleaned and sterilized multiple times. Labeling devices as single-use had more to do with OEMs' desire to sell more devices than any inherent fragility of the device. In some cases, what had been a reusable device one day became a single-use device the next.

In the US, the manufacturer gets to determine the materials used and the language on the label of any product they develop. The OEMs' analysis when making this decision should include whether there is a risk of sterility concerns, a risk of deterioration that could result in malfunction, or a risk of decreased efficacy.

The OEMs, unsurprisingly, took the natural course of focusing more on profit, and arbitrarily started labeling many devices "single-use" regardless of any actual risk. Whether the reclassification from reusable to SUD was the result of a need to limit liability or to protect a revenue stream was a point of argument in the 1960s or 1970s. But the manufacturers' motivation was evident if you followed the money trail.

For hospitals, relying on the OEMs' analysis and labeling meant that they had some inoculation against potential liability, as compared with having minimum-wage workers reprocess instruments in the hospital's own sterile processing department. Simply disposing of a SUD and not questioning whether it actually *could* be reprocessed was a win-win-win for everyone—the OEM, the hospital, and the salesman.

It actually got to the point that an external fixation device (XFIX)—attached on the outside of a patient's body and used to stabilize fractured bones, and typically made of stainless-steel bolts and carbon fiber rods—was labeled single-use!

Though poor technique was more often responsible for a negative patient outcome than a reprocessed instrument, when it came to the preferences of a highly paid surgeon versus the safety assurance provided by a minimum-wage reprocessing worker, perception was everything.

Then the 1980s came around, and diagnosis related groups (DRGs) were established as the basis of Medicare's hospital reimbursement system. The initial motive for developing DRGs was to create an effective framework for monitoring the quality of care and utilization of services in a hospital setting. Physicians and hospitals were no longer reimbursed on a cost basis and instead received a fixed procedure fee. Whether ten or ten thousand instruments were used in a procedure, the reimbursement from Medicare was the same.

The result? Medical devices, which had once been the second-highest surgical procedure cost to a hospital, suddenly needed to be trimmed. Facilities needed to take a very close look at their balance sheets. Even providers who had been vehemently opposed to using reprocessed SUDs were forced to reconsider a solution that would uphold patient outcomes, save them money, and support their environmental initiatives.

As a salesman, I had certainly played a role in and benefitted from the disposables boom, but the days of "billing the governor" were over. Hospitals were now responsible for their own costs and would no longer be so quick to order from salesmen like me. When private insurance companies followed Medicare's lead and moved over to a fixed-cost reimbursement policy, it was a perfect storm. Thanks to the advent of the materials manager—a role designed to ensure that hospitals were properly stocked and all purchasing decisions were effectively supervised to protect the bottom line—I knew that in order to survive, I needed to lower costs for the hospital. If I wanted to thrive, I needed to lower their costs *and* limit their liability.

I had done it once with surgical towels. Although EnviroMed was my greatest professional failure, the concept behind the business was sound. I knew in my gut that I could successfully reprocess more than just surgical towels. Other products *had* to be possible too. As I have said many times in my life—and come to regret more than a few—how hard could it be?

* * *

Among the salesman's most useful skills is an ability to read upside down, and this skill never served me better than during a meeting I had with Pam Cardwell. At the time, Pam was the director of central supply at St. Anthony's Hospital in St. Petersburg, Florida. As we sat talking in her office, my eye kept wandering to a suture package lying upside down on her desk. I couldn't get past the fact that the package looked larger than a suture package usually did.

Another useful skill for a salesman is the ability to think on his feet. With one ear on what Pam was saying and one eye on that package, I thought I was doing a decent job of splitting my focus. I could almost make out the name of the OEM printed across the bottom of—

Pam tossed the suture package at me. Taking her smirk and half smile as an invitation to look closer, I lifted the package and turned it the right way up in order to read the name: *Surgical Reprocessing Services, Inc.*, out of Texas.

It didn't make sense to me. During a surgical procedure, many times the outer portion of a suture package is removed in anticipation of the suture being used, but the internal seal is not broken if the suture is not used. For years, common practice in the Big Dog Kingdom had been for OEMs to replace the outer packaging for free.

"Why is the hospital paying to use this company," I asked, "when you can get it done for free?" I couldn't understand why, of all people, a materials manager would be willing to pay. Their margins were too tight for that.

"It's because of AIDS," Pam replied matter-of-factly. "The risk of contamination is too great, even for unused sutures, so the OEMs have stopped doing it."

I thought for a moment about all those sutures, still sterile and only in need of external resealing, repackaging, and terminal sterilization. We were talking about a proverbial sea of sutures no longer being reprocessed by the Big Dogs. The kingdom might have decided it no longer wanted the liability, but I knew the science—I knew how to reprocess without compromising anyone's safety. And if hospitals were already paying for the service, why wouldn't they pay *me* to do it?

Taking one last look at Pam, I determined then and there that if the OEMs no longer wanted to repackage and sterilize suture packs, I'd do it for them. I could sell them back to the same hospitals for a considerable discount on what it would cost for them to purchase new suture packs from the kingdom.

It was, therefore, the humble suture pack that started everything.

First, I needed capital. I would once again have to rely on my sales skills, but this time it was *my* potential, and not just the product that I was selling.

Although they were by now retired, I called my parents. My mother believed in my abilities, so she and my father agreed to lend me the twenty thousand dollars I somewhat timidly requested.

My brother Ted, by then a successful radiation oncologist, was my next call. He too agreed to lend me twenty thousand—but his willingness came with the stipulation that I had to promise I wouldn't move in with him if this venture didn't work out.

Marge had only accompanied me on sales calls once during my career, back when we were living in Durham. She found it stressful and exhausting—and more than a little annoying that people actually had the gall to tell me no, so she had never joined me again. For years she kept a comic strip on the fridge that showed a frazzled salesman, briefcase in hand, coming through a door, with the caption "I'm so happy to be home—I'm tired of being nice to people all day!" But she never forgot how eye-opening she had found my sales calls that day in Durham.

Marge had some innate selling skills herself, as she was able to convince two of her church friends to speak with their husbands about my plan. These two men had never even met me, yet each put in another twenty thousand dollars.

I bought a SteriJet machine from White Memorial Hospital in East Los Angeles for twenty thousand dollars. The machine used an ethylene oxide sterilization procedure. The product to be sterilized would be placed in a specialized plastic bag. The machine then created a vacuum, dispensed a dose of ethylene oxide, and immediately sealed the bag. The bag was then placed in a temperature-controlled room with a vent to the outside. Over a forty-eight-hour period, the gas evacuated through the bag, and the sterilization process was complete.

Before long, I was going around the Tampa Bay area, collecting suture packs whose outer packaging had been removed but whose original foil seal was still intact. All that I needed to do was repackage and sterilize the packs. Then I could sell them back to the hospitals for half the cost of a new suture pack. As a bonus, unnecessary medical waste wouldn't be going into the landfills, and thus hospitals saved the associated costs of handling that waste.

The Big Dogs did little more than lift their noses to the breeze created by my activity. What was there for them to be concerned about? We were just a husband-and-wife team who were renting six hundred square feet of space in a strip mall for $1,200 a month. Our reprocessing of suture packs posed no threat to the multibillion-dollar Big Dog Kingdom. But it wouldn't be long before they were barking ferociously from the porch.

Sutures represented just a small slice of the reprocessing market. The sterilization and repackaging process was exactly the same for other instruments that were opened but went unused during surgical procedures. The plastic bag we used for sterilizing sutures was eighteen inches wide by thirty-six inches long. Provided an instrument could fit in that bag, it could be sterilized. More and more often, we found ourselves filling the bag.

Some of our customers were pleased to see this uptick in our business. Nurses especially appreciated the savings to the hospital and the benefit to the environment. Quite possibly due to the nurturing aspect of their profession, many of them wanted to see us succeed. A typical conversation with a nurse went like this:

"Aren't you worried about the Big Dogs getting into the business and squashing you?" (The nurses were fully aware of the power of the kingdom.)

"There are three reasons," I replied, "why the OEMs are reluctant to do what we are doing." Then I would elaborate on those reasons.

First, space is at a premium in the surgical suite. Multiple collection containers for each manufacturer can't be accommodated.

Second, Vanguard's reject rate ran about 15 percent. We were highly motivated to reprocess and sell back as many devices as we could while upholding safety. We wouldn't get paid if the instrument was rejected.

The third, and probably most important reason, had to do with the kingdom cannibalizing its current revenue stream. If the Big Dogs reprocessed their products, that would reduce new-product sales. If they didn't, they would face Vanguard, who could save hospitals half the cost of a new device without compromising quality. The nurse in my hypothetical conversation faced a conundrum of her own. If a Big Dog rejected one of its own devices, how would she know whether it actually needed to be replaced? Who was to say that the device wasn't being rejected solely because the OEM preferred to sell the hospital a new one at full price? Unlike us, the Big Dogs had no real incentive to keep their rejection rate low. Every rejected reprocessed device meant that the client had no choice but to buy a brand-new device.

The decisions made by most of our customers were based on ethical reasons. I would watch as the nurse turned the information over in her mind, asking, *Will the manufacturers actually hurt themselves by reprocessing a device that they can sell for only half the price of a new one?*

* * *

The battleground that was emerging looked a lot like this: in the middle of a vast field is a house with a porch. Sleeping on that porch are dogs. They're big, the type of dogs homeowners keep for protection. Surrounding the house, yet set off at some distance, is a flimsy fence with a clear view through it to the world outside. But the big dogs generally have no need to keep watch over this fence. On the rare occasion some other animal gets too close, the fence prevents the dogs from having to tire themselves out by attacking this threat to their kingdom.

We were asking ourselves how they could come after us without damaging the fence. You see, the fence was the only thing that stood in the way of the Big Dogs wrapping their jaws around our necks.

So what to do? Would the pack mentality lead to the dogs barking furiously at us through the fence? Or would they come right through it, risking the integrity of their relationship with the hospital, who is their customer?

* * *

I have said it before: if you want to know the true motive, follow the money.

If you followed the money that Vanguard was bringing in at the time—fifty thousand dollars in our first year, as compared to several billion for the Big Dogs—it was easy to see how we were able to stay off their radar. That fifty thousand, however, told us everything we needed to know about the viability of Vanguard and of the reprocessing industry as a whole.

The day finally arrived when not only did we appear on the Big Dogs' radar, but did so with a large target on our back. I like to say that other guys don't care about what you're doing until you start drinking their beer and dancing with their women. Vanguard started drinking the kingdom's beer and dancing with their women with two products that we launched almost simultaneously: Electrophysiology (EP) catheters used to diagnose the part of the heart causing arrythmia and Gastrointestinal (GI) biopsy forceps used to take samples of the colon to determine the presence of disease

One afternoon, out of the blue, I got a call from Bill Stover, one of our reps in Arkansas.

"Hey Chuck," Bill said. "Can we reprocess EP catheters?"

"Sure we can," I replied. Then, my mind catching up to my mouth, I asked, "What's an EP catheter?"

These heart catheters are about as invasive a device as exists. They are used to electrically map the heart in order to determine which part is causing an arrhythmia, which is a problem with the rate or the rhythm of a patient's heartbeat. Up to that point, the EP catheters had been sold as reusable, with the instructions for reprocessing provided directly by the OEM.

Then the manufacturers made the decision to label the EP catheters as SUDs, but EP departments in hospitals throughout the US had ignored the label and continued to reprocess the catheters. In fact, when one hospital raised the alarm over the new single-use label, USCI Cardiology & Radiology Products, a division of C.R. Bard, sent a letter to this hospital that stated outright the catheter was the same product, the only difference being the label. Although the Medical Device Manufacturers Association (MDMA), a trade association that represented over 130 OEMs, asserted that the labeling decision was dependent on whether the device would expose a second patient "to an unreasonable and substantial risk of illness or injury," the letter said that the "manufacturing processes...have not changed. The electrodes are made with the same materials and in the same manner as they have been in the past."

Vanguard was fortuitous enough to get a copy of this letter. At every opportunity, we enthusiastically showed it to our customers, who were comfortable with us reprocessing their sutures but had qualms about us handling their EP catheters. The particular phrase we always made sure to point out was "with the same materials and in the same manner." Nothing about the product had changed from the time the hospitals had reprocessed the catheters themselves to the time we started offering to do the reprocessing for them.

Since reprocessing of EP catheters had been happening in hospitals for many years, the Big Dogs were still not overly alarmed by Vanguard, though they did get up to stretch and scratch a bit before dozing off once again. Vanguard's presence was starting to impact the quality of their sleep. We suspected that it was only a matter of time until they decided to take decisive action against us.

* * *

In 1995, right around the time Vanguard branched out into reprocessing EP catheters, we came across an article detailing an interview conducted with a marketer for Johnson & Johnson's contact lens company. The article included the marketer's admission that the contact lenses labeled "extended use" and the ones labeled "one-time use" were in fact the same product.

In April 2001, Johnson & Johnson was sued by multiple consumers. The accusation was that the company had been misleading customers, causing them to prematurely throw away Acuvue disposable contact lenses. The suit contended that the company intended to drive up sales of its more expensive one-day lenses, even though they knew the product was identical to its two-week lenses.

When a Johnson & Johnson marketer was asked why the company would do such a thing, he called it a business decision. It seems to have been a good one. Even after Johnson & Johnson settled the suit for $840 million in cash plus fees, a company spokesman deemed the settlement a "modest outlay."

For Vanguard, the existence of that article and the acknowledged profit motive behind how the Big Dogs were labeling their products was worth its weight in gold.

Not long after we learned about Johnson & Johnson's "business decision," another of the kingdom's dogs, Boston Scientific, the leading supplier of GI biopsy forceps, faced a decision of its own. GI biopsy forceps are used to take samples of the colon to determine the presence of disease. The forceps were sold as "hot," meaning that they had an electrical charge that allowed the physician to cauterize larger samples in order to prevent bleeding. The forceps could also be sold as "cold," and in that mode were used to remove smaller samples that didn't require cauterization.

At the time, Boston Scientific was selling the cold forceps for forty-five dollars and the hot forceps for seventy-five dollars. Altogether, forceps accounted for an annual revenue stream of approximately $200 million.

In 1993, Vanguard started reprocessing these instruments. I remember it like it was yesterday. I was sitting in my office, thinking about reprocessing EP catheters and GI biopsy forceps. I considered all the other devices that existed—some I didn't even know about, but that also could in all likelihood be reprocessed.

I was literally dizzy as all of those devices swirled in my head. I started calculating: biopsy forceps, laparoscopic instruments, sequential compression devices, pulse oximeter sensors, burrs, bits, and blades. I thought about the additional revenue streams we could open and envisioned the upward-sweeping curve of our annual sales. I calculated the savings we could offer our customers, consistent at fifty percent, no matter the device. I considered the vast amount of medical waste we could keep out of our landfills. As I sat in my office and gazed into the future, the possibilities were staggering. There was an entire landscape of devices out there just waiting to be reprocessed—a market waiting to change.

I didn't give it much thought at the time, but the Big Dogs were also waiting, their jaws capable of tearing us to shreds.

CHAPTER 8

THE WILD WEST

If you care about what people think about you, you will end up being their slave. Reject and pull your own rope.

— Auliq Ice

Along my road to starting Vanguard, one of the lines I picked up as a result of attending the AORN conference in Atlanta was with a company called Maxxim Medical. Based in Sugarland, Texas, Maxxim marketed custom procedure trays, which fell squarely in my wheelhouse. With the requirement that I had to retain one of Maxxim's independent reps, who would work for me, I was given a territory. I was so relieved to once again be selling that I didn't foresee the thorn in my side that this caveat would become.

In the aftermath of Johnson & Johnson's purchase of Sterile Design, unbeknownst to me, an old enemy arose. Jack Cahill came from Johnson & Johnson's Surgikos division to become the vice president of sales at Sterile Design. A few years later, Johnson & Johnson spun Sterile Design off to Maxxim Medical. Maxxim kept on some of the Sterile Design management team; one such holdover was Jack Cahill. Jack, whom I only knew by name, became my boss at Maxxim.

As I made my regular customer visits, what I failed to notice was that I was being asked more and more often whether everything was all right for me at Maxxim. Customers were concerned that something was going on between Jack and me. I didn't have the sense to stop and consider that anything could actually be amiss. From my perspective, the fall was behind me, and I was in my ascent.

Since I didn't really know him, I wasn't aware that Jack was a pretty hard-nosed operator, one with a long memory. I had sued Sterile Design after my blow-up with Dick Isel, and had gone to work for their biggest competitor, DeRoyal not long before Jack joined Sterile Design. He had not forgotten that, and evidently also was not willing to overlook it.

I, on the other hand, had put all that behind me. So, when I got the call to meet with Jack in his office, I thought it was great! I was finally making headway. He'd had time to see the level of sales I was making and, I assumed, intended to put me in a more important role. I thought, *He must want to give me the good news in person.*

When I walked into his office, Jack wasted no time in making it clear that I was not there to be promoted. "You're fired, Chuck," he said so matter-of-factly that I initially thought I had misheard him.

It seemed like an unfunny joke. But Jack's death stare made it clear that he wasn't kidding, and that I was an idiot for even considering that he might have been.

"But the territory—" I started.

"I'm giving it to your sub-rep," Jack replied, just as cold and as calm as could be. "And you're out."

I was so shocked that I don't remember if he actually gestured with his thumb toward the door, but I do recall that there wasn't enough time for me to reach an Isel-level of anger before finding myself on the other side of it. I wonder if my response sounded as meek as it felt when I said, "But Jack, I have a two-year contract."

Even in that moment, I was aware that his response was what he'd planned to say to me from the moment he was brought on by Maxxim. Though he may have delighted in saying it, his expression gave away nothing as he simply said, "Sue me."

Really? That was all I had the mental bandwidth to think as I numbly left his office.

The meeting couldn't have lasted longer than a couple of minutes, though the range of emotions it drew from me suggested an event—and a relationship with Jack—that was far more substantial. Jack never broke a sweat, since he knew I didn't have the funds to sue him. Although we have a great criminal legal system in this country, when it comes to civil cases, the guy with the biggest purse has the high ground. As Jack and I were both well aware, I had just found myself in the ditch.

It was a pleasant surprise as I was frantically running through my limited options, to discover that the cost of filing a lawsuit wasn't as high as I had anticipated. Thanks to Dave Galloway, the attorney I went shopping for in Plant City, I discovered that an affordable $120 would get the legal ball rolling.

"I don't have any money," I explained to Dave as we kicked off that first meeting. I had learned my lesson from my lawsuit against Sterile Design. The cost of filing is only the gateway to losing the shirt off your back; the true legal fees accumulate afterward.

Dave had a dry sense of humor and we had already decided that we liked each other. "Don't worry," he said. "You can pay as you go."

Under Dave's guidance, I first sued Maxxim in Florida under the Racketeer Influenced and Corrupt Organizations (RICO) Act. The jury found in my favor, but no damages were awarded. Dave, however, had always planned that if suing for racketeering didn't work out, we would sue again for breach of contract in Texas. Texas was where my contract as an independent representative had been established. More favorable laws existed there, including the potential for triple damages. In Texas, we took a second bite of the apple.

And bite we did. Although I couldn't disclose the details of the settlement, whenever someone asked me how things had turned out, I smiled and said, "Well, I have fifty thousand reasons to be happy."

It took five years and twenty thousand dollars in Dave's fees, but I eventually climbed out of that ditch ... alongside a new ally.

If there is one thing I have come to realize about my professional life, it is that allies may move in and out of my orbit, but they always remain within the same universe. These few people comprise a core group who've had the pleasure—or misfortune—of knowing two Chucks over the years. There was Pre-2000 Chuck and there is now Millennial Chuck. Even for my children, who arrived in pairs with four years between, childhood for the older pair was a vastly different experience than childhood was for the younger pair. Christine and Seth knew Pre-2000 Chuck. For Nathan and Joanne, I was the more relaxed Millennial Chuck.

Most of the people who worked with me at Vanguard remember Pre-2000 Chuck. As Nathan puts it, back then I was like a Jack Russell terrier who had to expend his energy or risk getting into trouble.

But here's the thing: a lot of fruit dies on the vine if you don't pick it. Being able to think quickly is helpful, but being able to make decisions quickly is crucial when you're running a business, especially if the business lives on the knife's edge of survival.

In any company, there will always be problems; it's just the nature of business. Vanguard faced additional complexities here and there, but no matter the number or nature of those challenges, someone had to come up with solutions. When you're the leader, that "someone" is you.

We often didn't have the luxury of time when it came to problem-solving. Although those experiences were stressful and high stakes, there were gifts to be found in the adversity we confronted together. In my opinion, the best thing you can do during a time of hardship is to actively determine to move forward. The "why" can be figured out later but moving forward should never stop. Many times, I *couldn't* stop. Moving forward was all I knew how to do. So, if I was antsy, it was in the name of not stopping.

The word "impatient" is often perceived as having a negative connotation, but I don't believe impatience and kindness are mutually exclusive. I'm described by others as quick, energetic, and engaging, but also kind and fair and honorable. I think my father would be proud of this assessment. People described Vanguard, especially in the early days, as being like a community, or even a family. Since everything always felt like it hung in the balance (because it did!), we relied on each other for support. We truly cared about one another, and worked with a singular purpose in mind, heart, and spirit, striving side by side for something we truly believed in. We were fiercely loyal, clinging together on a life raft.

Just as impatience and kindness can coexist, so hanging on for dear life and maintaining steadfast hope are not mutually exclusive.

Another thing people are nice enough to say about me is that I have a sense of humor. I can look back on the feedback I received when the company first started, compare it to what I heard from the same people when it was all over, and laugh heartily about the discrepancies. The initial reactions to my new ideas were largely pessimistic:

Why are you disregarding the odds?

You don't know what you're doing!

This is never going to work.

You're dealing with multibillion-dollar manufacturers—they'll kill you!

At the end of the road, these pessimistic predictions had become:

You're a genius!

You recognized this opportunity.

What a great job you did!

What an obvious moment it was in health care.

I suppose if I'm being honest with myself, there is some truth to be found in both perspectives. I'm grateful that at Vanguard I had people surrounding me who both fully supported me, and kept me accountable. I like to think that I did the same for them.

* * *

In 1991, Steve Bernardo was only nineteen years old. As he tells it today, he had two mentors in his career. Hugh was first, and I came next. Hugh owned a small accounting firm, and he gave Steve a shot at programming accounting software. Even though

Steve was still a college student, Hugh trusted him to work directly with some of the firm's clients, one of whom was a company called EnviroMed.

I don't remember Steve from my time at EnviroMed. It's likely that he and I never crossed paths, since I spent so much of my time out selling. His main contact at EnviroMed, and the person who signed his invoices without asking questions, was Doug Stante, the head of quality control at EnviroMed. During break times, Doug could usually be found sitting out back of the building with a Diet Pepsi in one hand and a cigarette in the other. On those occasions when Hugh accompanied Steve to EnviroMed, the three of them would end up outside, shooting the breeze for quite a bit longer than was necessary or, in all likelihood, appropriate.

Steve might not have known it at the time, but it was probably a relief for Doug to get out of the building. He surely needed to take a frequent break from the craziness that was going on inside company walls. Doug's wife was the sister of Tom Howard's wife, so Doug wasn't just working *with* his brother-in-law—he was actually working *for* his brother-in-law. I don't think many people envied his predicament.

Doug knew that I'd been fired by Tom and the board. Maybe he suspected, or came to suspect that I had been *unfairly* fired, because he soon found himself in the same position of being unceremoniously let go, thanks to Tom Howard. Losing my job may have been tough, but at least I didn't have to endure the awkward family get-togethers I imagine Doug did.

Steve was disappointed when he found out about Doug's firing from EnviroMed, as was Hugh. The accounting firm had just come into possession of a brand-new laser printer, so Hugh, who wanted to do something to help, let Doug know that he was welcome to print his resumés on the new printer. This benefit alone couldn't have been the reason that Doug took Hugh up on the offer—because Doug ended up coming into the office every day for an entire year! He didn't do much more than hang out, smoke cigarettes, and play long hours of a flight simulator video game. But Steve and Hugh got used to seeing him there. When the day eventually came that Doug *didn't* show up, Hugh grew concerned. Anxious, he made a phone call.

"Hey Doug," Hugh said, trying to keep the alarm out of his voice. "You okay? You didn't come in today."

Steve was listening to the conversation from right behind Hugh's shoulder and heard Doug say he was fine but was now "hanging out somewhere else."

That "somewhere else" was at Vanguard, with me.

Unlike the time he spent at the accounting firm, when Doug was at Vanguard, he did more than smoke cigarettes and play video games. He worked, and he worked hard!

Not only that, Doug didn't actually get paid for that work. I never misled Doug about this fact. When I offered him the job of heading up quality assurance and regulatory affairs, I made it clear that I couldn't pay him a salary. Steve still finds it funny that I was able to lure Doug away from spending time with him and Hugh, and jokes that I must have doubled his nonexistent salary.

I did promise that when money came in, I would look after Doug. His reasoning for coming over to join me—sorry, Steve—was, in his own words, that he had nothing better to do. How much of a risk was he really taking when he already wasn't earning any money? Doug was intrigued when I explained what we were doing and was more than happy to work with Marge and me. Marge's role was as office manager, secretary, customer service manager, and whatever else was required of her in the course of a typical day. There was no money to pay any of us. Not to mention that she left her workday only to go home and put in a second shift with the kids and the running of the household.

Also working at Vanguard at this time was Vicky Kennedy. Vicky was our first production worker and Vanguard's first paid hire. Vicky was the mother of Nathan's best friend and a friend of Marge's from the PTA. Vicky had mentioned that she was looking for some part-time work, so Marge introduced her to me. Such a personal relationship might have been difficult to navigate in any other workplace, but at Vanguard our every connection soon came to be recognized as a source of strength.

Doug recalls that it was while he was over at my house helping me with my car's brakes when I asked him to work with me at Vanguard. Along with being able to fix almost anything, Doug had a mind like a steel trap. He had been an aviation technician during his time in the Marines, before moving into quality assurance and avionics. In that field, he gained a solid technical troubleshooting background. His love of systematic problem-solving must have made the prospect of working at Vanguard very compelling for him to go without pay for as long as he did. I tell anyone who will listen that I'm not really into details—a statement people who know me will readily agree with—but Doug was meticulous. He lived for the details. Even when we played Duke Nukem, Doug was fastidious—he designed and built a game map that was an exact replica of the Vanguard building layout.

We would all show up at the plant around eight o'clock on a Saturday morning, ready to dig into whatever work had been left over after the preceding sixty-hour workweek. "Why don't we play Duke Nukem a bit," I'd suggest, "just to get it out of our system."

Around three hours later, when lunchtime was approaching, someone would say, "Let's get some pizza and then get right to work."

Shooting virtual weapons at one another proved extremely therapeutic for us all. When we eventually got around to working— around two or three in the afternoon—we were able to relax and re-engage.

It was after a year of working at Vanguard that Doug remembers finally receiving a paycheck—just enough for his monthly car payment. I have always preferred that people be compensated what they're worth, but Doug thankfully saw the promise in Vanguard and trusted that he would eventually see a return on his investment. He also knew that I was maxed out on all my personal credit cards and had squeezed out every penny of equity in my house.

I'll never forget the simple Christmas meal that bonded all of us together. We had to be thrifty, so Doug, his wife Bridget, Marge, and I sat together over a meal of homemade lasagna. We raised glasses of unpretentious wine to the future, and I'm certain we all made similar wishes for success and prosperity as we watched the single candle on the small dessert cake flicker.

With Doug spending such long hours at Vanguard, it wasn't long before he introduced me to Steve. It was 1992, and with the volume of sutures we were doing, we needed a system on the back end; pen and paper weren't going to cut it for much longer. It wasn't a lot of work, maybe ten weekends in total, for Steve to put together an inventory-management program for us, but he was happy to be in touch with Doug again and seemed excited about the chance to build something independently.

Luckily for me, this translated into a willingness to work for free. Maybe Steve was also willing because, as he acknowledges now, he fully expected to fail. If that eventuality came to pass, Steve assumed that he and I would both move on, the only loss being a few wasted weekends.

Steve, however, proved to be an extraordinarily capable programmer. My decision to rely on Steve was as simple as taking Doug's recommendation to allow him to try. Of course, it didn't hurt that we were able to afford the free help Steve was willing to provide!

Even once some time had passed after implementing the inventory-management program—time during which he continued to study at the University of South Florida and work for Hugh—Steve wasn't sure how I felt about the programming he had done for Vanguard. Many months later, Doug invited Steve over to the Vanguard lunchroom, where we usually ate our Burger King sandwiches. Steve was still young, about twenty or twenty-one by this time, and his rate was up to an affordable amount for us, about eight dollars an hour. When he found out we were still using his suture program—so regularly that we needed some changes made to it—he was surprised but once again willing to put in programming time after hours.

His gig started out as approximately ten hours a week. Steve still likes to tell the story—he gets a kick out of mentioning the very obviously outdated technology involved. He did the work from his bedroom in his mother's house, mostly in the evenings after class or when his work with Hugh was over for the day. He transmitted his output over the phone line to my office computer. Using a pager, he would let me know to leave my office computer on that night when I went home, because he was planning to transmit. Or, I would page him during the day and he'd call me back when he had a break, so I could tell him about changes I wanted him to make. It may not have been a pretty way to operate, but it definitely worked for us.

Little did Steve know at the time, but his program, which used the Magic programming language, would turn into his life's work. He eventual rose to become the vice president of information technology and make $100,000 a year at Vanguard, but he derived his true pleasure from the lifespan of this program, which grew exponentially in size and complexity. He considered those sixteen years of effort his greatest professional accomplishment.

It's bittersweet to Steve that he was given such an incredible opportunity so early in his career—an opportunity that would never be repeated. He likes to say that he spent a good part of his early adulthood wishing I was his father, and I acted as if I really were his father as well as his boss.

As a teenager, my son Seth was looking to make some money, so he came to work with us. It didn't take long for Seth and Steve to bond, but there were some painful life lessons Seth had to learn. At the time, he had an earring and wore his hair in a long ponytail. Seth and Christine's nickname for me was Attila the Hun due to my authoritative parenting style, but my only concern about the earring and the hairstyle was as they related to the company. We were trying to sell customers on reprocessed medical devices, a practice that gave many people immediate cause for concern due to hygiene. We had to be very cautious about how we presented ourselves.

"It's a reality of life," I said to Seth, "that people make judgments based on looks."

"It's not fair, Dad," he replied.

"I get it. I know it's not fair, but that's how it is. I can't allow it here."

"I'm not doing it."

"Okay. Then don't do it."

At sixteen, however, Seth decided he wanted money more than he wanted long hair and an earring. I made him an offer of four dollars an hour, at a time when the going rate was five to six dollars.

He cut his hair, removed his earring, and accepted my offer. "I get paid every two weeks, right?" he asked.

"Yes, every two weeks."

"So that's $320?"

"Yes, eighty hours of work is $320."

Two weeks later, Seth received his first paycheck. I knew because he came into my office looking pretty upset.

"Dad, I thought you said I would be paid $320?"

"That's right," I responded.

"Well, then why am I getting less than that?" he asked, exasperated. "And who is FICA?"

I just had to smile.

Though he started off emptying the trash cans and handling other janitorial tasks, Seth's natural curiosity and sharp mind made his rise through the ranks inevitable. He credits me with giving him his foundation of faith and Doug with awakening his confidence, as Seth eventually worked very closely under Doug in quality assurance and regulatory affairs.

Nathan, at age fifteen, joined his older brother in the warehouse. Before long, he too quickly moved into helping out with whatever was needed around the office. Thanks to his long-running interest in computers, he built the first Vanguard website and eventually worked in the IT department with Steve. Steve was eventually a groomsman at Nathan's wedding. And Steve has long been considered to be, and is still referred to by the Masek family as, the "fifth child."

It was important to Marge and me that the boss's kids weren't seen as getting preferential treatment. Being the boss's son was Seth's greatest on-the-job stressor. It troubled him to no end that he might never earn respect that wasn't tied to me. It was around this time that Seth stopped calling me "Dad" or even "Father", at work. Although the roots of this change lie in the psychological challenge he faced as the oldest son working under his father, I think we both took a measure of pride in it. He earned it. He proved himself.

Every day could easily have been Vanguard's last, and we started every morning under the weight of a heavy question mark. Yet we always ran the company as if it were a much bigger operation. As a result, neither Seth nor Nathan ever reported directly to me. This separation was as important or more important to them than it was to me, and I respected it. I wanted them to work on their own and answer for that work independent of their relationship to me.

If anything, I may have been tougher on Seth and Nathan than on any other employee, including Steve, who was closest to them in age. Nathan worked for Millennial Chuck, and he wasn't bothered by my toughness, since he felt he was being looked after in other ways. Seth, though, worked for Pre-2000 Chuck, and as a result needed to wear multiple hats, even some that he considered ill-fitting. I quite often needed Seth to handle menial company tasks or act as gopher. One of these tasks, even after he had worked his way up in quality assurance, was to pick up business visitors at the airport. He was literally that guy in arrivals whom you see uncomfortably holding up a little sign bearing a stranger's name and making eye contact with no one. Oh, how Seth hated that job!

It's interesting, however, the benefit that perspective gives. Whereas Seth viewed the responsibility of meeting people at the airport as a punishment, I saw the job as an important one, since our visitors were doctors and nurses. It required me to put a lot of trust in him.

One of Seth's best memories—not just of Vanguard, but of me as his father and as a man—is of when he was in the midst of writing a thesis for college. Seth was about fifty-five pages into it when I called him for help. I had a meeting at Tampa General Hospital and had forgotten my cardiac catheter demo product. Seth tore himself away from his work to take the call, but hung up with the "Aw, man" feeling about having to yet again be my gopher.

Nevertheless, he got in the car and drove out to meet me. The hospital, even back then, was huge. Seth parked out front and waited for me to exit the building. Apparently, when I emerged, I looked remarkably small in comparison to the building towering behind me. I was wearing a suit and was otherwise well prepared for the meeting, but Seth was taken by how I had to turn around and walk back into that big building and make even bigger things happen for the company. It was a moment, he says, when he felt a deep respect for my work and an appreciation for how doing it couldn't have been easy for me.

The need to protect Marge from constant threats to our finances was an unspoken Masek family agreement. She is a warrior, but also a self-confessed *worrier*. We all knew that her hard-earned nest was her sanctuary, and we decided not to invade it with talk of the ebbs and flows that passed over us quickly, but would likely linger in Marge's mind and cause her significant concern.

It had been a great relief to her when we finally settled into our country home on Bruton Road, just north of Plant City. Not only did this home base allow the roots of Vanguard Medical Concepts to grow, but it also allowed her the opportunity to devote a good deal of energy to the early years of its development. In God's timing, having a steady home base meant that we and all four of our children could be an integral part of the company in its formative years. Marge knew that a family saga was being created, one that was bound up with coworkers pulling together to build a company whose vision held the promise of making the world a better place. But in order to do that, Vanguard had to survive.

After EnviroMess had clobbered our finances and my self-esteem, I joked with Marge that if we ever clawed our way out from under $250,000 in debt, we'd call it a draw. I was sincere, however, when I made the promise that I would never again put her in the position of having to be concerned that she might lose her home. Protecting my wife from the threats that seemed to accumulate on a daily basis in business was a truce I considered myself fortunate to make.

I tell people all the time, "If you see footprints on my wife, trust me when I tell you that they're not mine." No other woman would have stayed with me after what I put Marge through. I knew it then, and I have never forgotten it since! So, while the agreed-upon policy when it came to Vanguard was "don't ask, don't tell," I have never lost sight of the fact that I was blessed to have my wife's support. I would do anything to protect the trust she had in me to always stay true to our deal.

CHAPTER 9

FIXED TO CENTER

If you want to go fast, go alone. If you want to go far, go together.

— African proverb

When Mark Salomon broke away from Johnson & Johnson—the biggest of the kingdom's Big Dogs—he was given one month's pay for every year he had worked at the company. Finding himself in the position of having sixteen months to go out and reinvent himself, Mark picked up a few lines. One of those lines brought him into Pam Cardwell's office.

"You need to meet Chuck Masek, my friend," Pam said. "Have you ever met or heard of him?"

"No, don't know him," Mark responded.

"Well, you two are a lot alike. And Chuck could really use somebody like you. So, here's his number."

I'm not sure what Mark's expectations were, but true to the nature of a salesman, he was pretty relentless about trying to make contact with me. He called Vanguard three times, and three times his number ended up in my trash can. Although Pam was a mutual friend, the only thing I knew about Mark was that he worked for Ethicon, Johnson & Johnson's suture division. And not just worked there—Mark was the product director responsible for all repackaging and sterilization in that high-earning division. Mark was clearly the enemy, so why would I want to talk with him? His job was to put me out of business.

Ethicon no longer wanted to spend the $4 million per year it cost them to resterilize and ship repackaged sutures back to their customers, which had been a free service for years. The AIDS epidemic and risk of blood-borne pathogens were making some OEMs nervous, but Mark knew that Ethicon's real reason for wanting to get out of reprocessing sutures came down to money. As part of his role, Mark had presented his research into the issue of reprocessing to Ethicon's senior management team.

Five lawyers asked him why Vanguard shouldn't or couldn't reprocess when there already existed a precedent in the industry for reprocessing devices. Mark knew that the lawyers were right. Legally, Ethicon, didn't have a leg to stand on. How could they stop us from doing what they and the other OEMs had been doing for decades?

The fourth time Mark called, he decided to ask if he could speak to someone other than me, and Doug ended up being that someone.

The conversation they ended up having was, for Doug anyway, eye-opening. "Oh wow, really? Oh *wow*," he kept repeating. I can't pretend that I wasn't a little curious. "I know Chuck will want to talk to you," I heard him say. I groaned inwardly at the prospect.

Despite my apprehension about dealing directly with a Big Dog, this time Mark's number didn't end up in the trash can.

A few days later, I met Mark for lunch at Buddy Freddys, a popular restaurant in Plant City. The running joke was that once I find a place I liked, there is nowhere else I (along with Doug, Mark, Dave McElhaney, and Jeff Schroeder, who referred to themselves as "Chuck's Boys") would go to eat. At the time, Buddy Freddys, was that place. As is almost always the case, I finished my meal first. Mark was doing his best to answer the questions I was firing at him between bites. When I realized he was no longer with Ethicon, I wasn't subtle about picking his brain about how Ethicon had done their reprocessing, and what they knew about us and how we did ours. Based upon what Mark was sharing, Vanguard was no longer just a nuisance to be ignored. We were starting to nip at the Big Dogs' heels.

Finally, Mark decided he was done answering my questions and wasn't shy about saying so. "Enough of this chitchat. Here's the bottom line: I like what you're doing. I want to sell it. If you're going to make this company what you say it's going to be, then you need to go back inside and let me take over sales in your territory."

With a simple "Okay," Mark became a member of the family. Together we would learn why it is said that you should let sleeping dogs lie.

If you were to ask Mark today, he'd no doubt say that I have slowed down a lot since the early days. During Mark's first years at Vanguard, however, the pace at which we worked was equally frenetic. Everyone remembers Mark and his Previa, the van that he drove all over the Tampa Bay area to pick up used medical devices from hospitals. All of the seats had been removed, so he would come back with that van filled from floorboard to ceiling with devices to be reprocessed.

Doug was back at the plant, working in what Mike Mayry, who would come to head up West Coast sales, referred to as his bunker. Doug made sure that whatever we reprocessed would actually be accepted by the hospitals. Although from day one we operated as a legitimate medical device operation, we faced some obstacles—like no running water in the production room! The single source of water was in the bathroom, so Doug did a lot of carrying a tub back and forth.

Doug clearly recalls the first product he had to figure out a way to clean: the GI forceps. None of us will ever forget the process he developed. He filled the tub with water, then stood back and watched as all this gunk slowly oozed out of the forceps. Much of the time, because the necessary equipment wasn't sold on the market, Doug was charged with figuring out not only how to clean a device, but how to design and build the cleaning vessel itself.

We all fondly recall a particularly memorable experiment that involved a fair-size pressure cooker. This of course was back in the days when you could buy a pressure cooker without bringing Homeland Security to your door. Doug drilled half-inch holes all the way around the pressure cooker's base, approximately thirty of them, and staggered them so that the cooker wouldn't crack when pressurized. Rubber stoppers were used to secure the biopsy forceps, which were coiled up inside the cooker. Their jaws were pushed through so that only the very end of the forceps was sticking out through the stoppers. The hardest part wasn't the jaws, which had serrated teeth. What almost killed us were stoppers. After inserting the forceps, there remained several holes in the rubber stoppers that we knew needed to be plugged. For this purpose, we purchased flathead nails. Then we sealed the lid and brought the cooker to pressure.

We had to be sure that we physically cleaned the forceps, ensure that the data supported that fact, and verify that the entirety of the complicated device was sterile as a result of our cleaning process. On this day, we also had to duck. When that pressure cooker reached pressure—and we probably should have anticipated this—the nails shot out of it like bullets!

After a quick inspection of one another and verbal confirmations that we were all unhurt, Doug realized that he had discovered the suitability of pressure for cleaning intricate devices. His design was later propagated in a number of cleaning systems in the reprocessing industry. Even to this day, there are custom manufacturers who use Doug's basic concepts for pressurized cleaning of reusable instruments.

Drying was another story. An instrument could appear clean and be proven to be clean, but making sure that it remained that way through and after drying was another problem entirely. To solve this problem, Doug demonstrated his usual genius and came up with a forced-air system that essentially blew air through the devices. It operated a bit like some sort of hokey hairdryer, but it did the trick. I look back fondly, though somewhat skeptically, at the degree to which we were sailing the ship even as we were building it.

A shared characteristic of the early Vanguard employees was how far we had all strayed from our intended careers. I was the microbiologist CEO, Doug was heading up quality and operations with a degree in marketing, and Mark had a degree in accounting as head of sales and marketing. Though we were a motley cast of characters, the benefit of so many people not being experts in the roles they assumed was that no one was overly territorial or married to their way of doing things. We were figuring it out together and stepping up as needed to offer whatever we believed we could. As Mark once said, knowing nothing also meant that no one had to be trained out of any bad habits.

I was the evangelist, working with hospitals to dispel the myths surrounding reprocessing and cultivating confidence in the scientific method that ensured its safety. All the while, I was racking up personal credit card debt as I tried to keep the lights on. Mark was picking up used devices and delivering reprocessed, sterile devices back to area hospitals. Doug, with Seth's help, built our ventilation system from scratch to ensure that no one would succumb to fumes.

In this sense, when Mark describes himself, Doug, and me as the "Three Amigos," he is correct. We may have been unlikely messengers, but the medical revolution we were about to inspire would soon take hold in a way that no one, especially the Big Dogs, could ever have predicted.

I had to sell the Vanguard vision to our customers, but when it came to our employees, I didn't need to do any convincing that reprocessing was the right road to take. "It's the right thing to do" became our simple company slogan, one rooted in science. As such, it didn't take long for the mantra to become inscribed in people's hearts and minds.

For this, I cannot take credit. Leaders are simply people who are willing to say, *"We're going this way."* I made the decision that we would go where the science led us. I consider myself fortunate that the individuals who joined me believed in what we were doing, and to this day feel proud of their participation.

One metaphor that describes how my decisions drove the company's vision can be found in the structure of an atom. An atom has a positively charged nucleus, where the bulk of the mass is found. Surrounding that nucleus is a dispersed cloud of negatively charged electrons. The electrons are bound to the nucleus by an electrostatic force far greater than that of gravity. Although the strength of our bonds in Vanguard would be tested over and over, and by increasingly powerful external forces, the binding mass at the core of Vanguard was truly the science. What ultimately connected us to one another and to doing the right thing had its basis in science. With solid science as our foundation, we all gained confidence from knowing that we would always do the right thing, no matter what pressures we faced.

Bowing to the facts wasn't always easy. Doug and I had a deep respect for each other. He always understood that my view was necessarily broader than his; I always recognized that his meticulousness put me in a position to be able to look toward the future. We had to navigate a challenging push and pull between our roles. Doug appreciated that we needed revenue streams from new products in order to survive, but he also understood that, just like him, I couldn't move from the scientific foundation and could not ignore the data. I pushed him hard, and there were times when I found it equally challenging when his natural reaction was to pump the brakes.

Our discussions about whether a new product could be reprocessed went something like this. I would open with "We need to get this clean."

"Can't do it," Doug would reply.

"Make it happen."

"We can't get it clean."

"Get it *done*, Doug."

"Not gonna happen."

At times, it felt like we were talking *at* each other.

He was usually right. I could direct him all I wanted, but if the science said it wasn't possible, it wasn't going to happen.

Acquiescing was extremely difficult for me, and it never really got any easier. My job was to get results. Doug's job was to allow the results to speak for themselves. Neither of us could argue against the science, because at Vanguard science always won. It wouldn't take us long, however, to discover that not all of our competitors prioritized patient safety over profit.

With hindsight, the fact that our employees witnessed our struggle between profitability and safety was likely one of the factors that strengthened the Vanguard bond and made people believe they were working for the right team. This faith meant that I could challenge people and push them really hard. I respected their talents, which gave them the confidence to stand their ground, even when the data wasn't there. I know it now, and though there were times when it was hard to admit it, I knew it then. No one was actually pumping the brakes; they were all helping to steer the car. We didn't know our final destination, or even the route we needed to take to get there, but we were blessed to share a compass that remained true.

Trust means believing in something, whether or not scientific verification is possible. We all trusted in the notion that there was something going on that was bigger than all of us. When you approach work, relationships, and life with the philosophy that you should live as a person who is centered, yet never try to delude yourself into believing that you *are* the center, rigidity and dogmatism cease being concerns. When you're truly centered, although it may seem counterintuitive, you possess an innate ability to be flexible. You find yourself capable of shifting *because* you are fixed on the right thing.

As with any business, I hired some employees who weren't a good fit for the company. These were the people who couldn't adapt to an environment that required immense flexibility. As we liked to joke, these were the individuals who couldn't learn to live in the eye of the shit storm. When you're rigid, you run the risk of being dogmatic. Rigidity breeds arrogance and pride about your own knowledge and makes you unresponsive to other perspectives— even when that perspective is scientifically sound and not bound to ego. Not everyone was aligned with the notion that there was some sort of authority beyond themselves at work within Vanguard. As a result, those people didn't stick around for very long.

Jeff Schroeder sold his small CPA firm near Orlando, then moved into our Bruton Road home for the first two or three months that he worked as Vanguard's CFO. He made the nearly two-hour drive home to Orlando on the weekends, but during the week he put in twelve-hour days with me, and we'd head back to the house together. After Marge made us dinner, we'd settle on the couch to watch the news. Within a couple of moments, she would turn to ask us a question and realize that we had already fallen asleep. Then we would get up the next morning and do it all over again.

Not everyone could maintain this same level of fortitude. I was just a man who had to feed his family, so my perseverance was born out of need. I can't judge others who struggled with the relentless intensity, for those were some tough days. I simply had no other choice but to stay the course. It amazes me to look back on what we did, but when you're going through it, you keep going.

Through the years we saw a few of our employees' handle job and life stresses in other ways. Jeff recalls one young woman who worked in the accounting office whose name he can't remember, which suggests just how brief her tenure at Vanguard was. As the story goes, she said she was going out for lunch one day, and didn't come back. To the best of everyone's knowledge, she was never seen at the company again.

I had a more personal experience with another short-term employee, a receptionist whom I had to fire for improper use of the company credit card. I came in one morning to find an unexplained $500 charge on the card, so I asked her if she had any idea who could be responsible. She was shocked and proceeded to spend the next few days trying to discover which employee could possibly have had such a lapse in moral judgment as to steal from the company. Finally, and unexpectedly, the receptionist broke down in tears in my office and admitted that she was in fact the culprit—she'd fallen behind on her car payments, and she hadn't known what else to do. She was humiliated and sincerely sorry for what she'd done, but I had to terminate her. I told her that had she come to me, we could have worked something out. I'd likely have been able to help her, but now I had no choice but to let her go.

It fell on Henry Philpot, director of human resources, to walk this extremely emotional young woman out of the building. I fired her, and having to fire someone is one of the hardest things a leader has to do. I wouldn't fully learn how gut-wrenching terminating people could be until years later, when the Vanguard family was much larger and even more interconnected.

Just as I never intended to build a company that would disrupt a multibillion-dollar industry, I never sought to start a family business. The irony in this statement makes me chuckle, because the word most used by former employees to describe the atmosphere in Vanguard is "family." At one time or another, Marge and each of our children worked at Vanguard. Seth and Nathan used their time there as a jumping-off point for careers in the medical device industry. Christine became highly credentialed in accounting, and

Joanne in nursing. The idea that I was never looking to "do the family business" is humorous.

My goal, as I told Mark one day, was to build something solid that would also ultimately sell. Mark, with his OEM sales-training credentials, recognized my intention as a sign that Vanguard was going to "go gangbusters."

But to achieve this, we needed to stay alive. Seth had to stand at the airport with a little sign. Henry had to walk a just-fired, sobbing woman to her car. Mark, who at Ethicon had boasted the most customers in the state of Florida, had to drive around to local hospitals in a jerry-rigged van. And Doug spent the bulk of his time at Scotty's Hardware.

As for me, I gained a reputation for punching numbers into a calculator as I sat with employees, making projections of what their shares in the company would buy them when Vanguard sold—kids' college funds, a mortgage-free home.

In order to make everyone money, the company had to be saleable. And in order to stay alive long enough to sell it, I had to make some deals that I was well aware were not optimal. As the leader, these were decisions that I needed to make.

We had an eclectic mix of neighbors near our location on Alsobrook Street, including a jeweler and a tractor supply store. We all shared a common landlord, Mike. I decided to approach him for a loan. With the original investors' $120,000 dwindling, and my credit cards maxed out, Vanguard had to raise some cash fast.

The deal Mike offered was not a good one: $100,000 at 18 percent interest. Since legally he couldn't charge us a higher interest rate, we verbally agreed that he would also buy stock for a dollar, and Vanguard would buy it back for $22,000 after one year. At the same time, the other $118,000 would be due in full. There's little doubt that this was a bad deal, and Marge bears what many people might consider a justified grudge against Mike to this day.

"Chuck, that's not fair," she complained, when I told her.

"I know, honey," I said with sincerity. "It *isn't* fair."

But we did pay back $140,000 on that $100,000 loan just one year later. I have never wavered in my belief that it was the right thing to do. Without that deal, we wouldn't have been able to keep our doors open.

"Bootstrapping" doesn't come close to describing how lean Vanguard was running. I was greeted every morning by a neat mound of dust beside one of my desk's legs—thanks to the termites that had come with our twenty-dollar investment in this secondhand piece of furniture. Although it seemed like my desk was constantly in danger of falling apart, we knew our adherence to the scientific method and to the most stringent safety practices was our most important investment and would soon start to pay dividends.

In the meantime, Mark appreciated that he didn't have to carry the devices very far on his multiple daily product drop-offs and pickups. (However, he still blames his bad back on all the boxes he hauled back and forth.) We started off in a single six hundred square foot space, labeled number 2. We soon began gobbling up additional spaces as they became available. They were reminiscent of office spaces in a strip mall, but we always referred to them as "buildings." When someone called for me, for instance, Vicky might tell them I was in building 4 and would get back to them in a few minutes. There was no need for anyone to know that those buildings were only a few feet apart, or that we'd had to run a network cable out the back to connect them—a cable that soon was struck by lightning.

Around this time, Robin Wilson earned a microbiology degree and was starting her first job at a very small company in Lakeland. That company, Encore, was owned by Dr. Kevin Browne, who was doing some interesting work with balloon angioplasty catheters in a three-room facility with a total of eight employees. At the time, Robin didn't know much about reprocessing devices beyond the balloon catheter, but she was hired by Encore to do production, cleaning, processing, and quality control inspection. She'd been a lab rat for about a year when she found out Vanguard was purchasing Encore. We bought the company with stock, and we gained some technology that we hoped would validate the reprocessing we were doing. We also gained Robin, who interviewed with Doug for a position in our quality assurance department.

Several years later we decided to get out of the balloon angioplasty catheter business. It was a Class III device that required more time and money then we felt it was wise to spend. Nonetheless, what we got from Encore and our effort to understand the balloon process positioned us to be more attractive to our next round of investors. Much to Marge's relief, cash from those investors paid off the $140,000 we owed to Mike.

* * *

I had lost track of Bill Frisbey since the days when he trained me at Travenol. He was about to re-enter my orbit and open what seemed like an entire universe of hospitals for Vanguard. He'd never lost his networking touch, and he maintained some unbelievable relationships with people at Florida Hospital in Orlando (now known as AdventHealth Orlando).

One of Bill's contacts, who I was particularly interested in getting to know, was involved in Princeton Investments, a division of Florida Hospital. We knew we had the science behind us. We also knew that the science wasn't enough—that without additional investment we would die. Even if another deal did come along, it would have similar terms to Mike's, and wouldn't provide enough cash. The stakes for Vanguard were higher than ever.

Representatives from Princeton toured our facility on Alsobrook. Had anyone asked, I would have told them that the boxes they were looking at, already labeled with the names of hospitals and products, were in fact empty. We knew those orders would come eventually. But thanks to the hospital's investment of $500,000—and the board seat with a $125,000 annual salary we gave to Bill as head of sales—it wasn't going to take as long as we'd thought.

* * *

"If the parking lot is this pretty," Marge said from the passenger seat, looking around at the oak-dotted expanse as I pulled our car into a shady spot, "can you imagine what the inside looks like?"

We were bursting at the seams on Alsobrook Street, and badly needed to find new premises. The building for rent on Great Oak Drive in Lakeland offered five times the amount of space we had on Alsobrook.

As if reading my mind, Marge said, "How are we ever going to fill all this?"

In that fifteen thousand square feet of space, I thought, we can roller skate—if we ever get the time.

The Big Dogs didn't know what was going on inside the Vanguard plant and made emotional appeals to customers, suggesting we were undoubtedly nefarious. When news of our reprocessing of hot and cold GI biopsy forceps reached Microvasive, a division of Boston Scientific, their response was one of the worst management decisions they could have made—and laid the groundwork for the battle Vanguard would soon face.

Microvasive's first instinct when they learned we were reprocessing these devices, new sales of which accounted for a $200 million dollar annual revenue stream, was not to increase the price on the forceps, but instead lower the price. Since our fee to the hospital customer was 50 percent of the cost of a new device, then every time that OEM lowered their price, our price followed. The Big Dogs could cut and cut and cut, and only hurt themselves.

As a result of their brilliant strategy, Boston Scientific took their $200 million market down to just $80 million over the next ten years. Our net profit percentage remained the same. We were effectively functioning as a laundry service for the hospitals, so our position couldn't have been better. If the OEMs represented Goliath, we were David, and the hospital clients stood on the battlefield between us. We were able to hide behind those hospitals while we served them. To get to us, Goliath had to make the decision to eventually kill their own market.

Lowering prices was a costly move that the OEMs were determined not to repeat. If they were going to stop us in the future, they realized they needed a different way to do it. Unfortunately for us, they soon found several.

Smith & Nephew, was a large medical technology company based in the UK. Their orthopedic division specializes in joint replacement systems for knees, hips, and shoulders. They also happened to sell arthroscopic shavers that we started to reprocess in the mid-nineties.

Unbeknownst to us, they had gone into one of our hospitals and convinced someone to hand over some of the devices we'd reprocessed. If it hadn't been for one of our investors, Peter Weiss, we would never have known how close we came to being killed. Peter was a German national who owned a company called World of Medicine, an OEM supplier of devices for minimally invasive procedures. He made arthroscopic pumps that attached to Smith & Nephew's shavers. Saline was pumped through the knee to help remove surgical debris in order for the surgeon to better see the meniscus.

Peter, fortuitously for us, had a friend who owned a testing lab in Tuttlingen, Germany. One day, this friend called Peter. Peter learned that his friend was in receipt of seven reprocessed arthroscopic shavers from Vanguard that Smith & Nephew had sent to his lab. He had tested the devices as requested and was sorry to share the results with Peter: all seven devices were found to be contaminated.

As a concerned investor, Peter called me shortly thereafter. "Who sent them?" I asked.

The answer didn't surprise me: "Smith & Nephew."

Around the same time, we received notice that Loma Linda University Health System in California had been given some of our reprocessed shavers. Smith & Nephew asked the university's orthopedic department to do a study on the shavers and publish that study.

Because I believe that there is no such thing as luck, my brother Ted being married to a woman whose maiden name is Slater cannot possibly be considered serendipitous. Call it fate, call it providence, call it what you will—but my sister-in-law's father, Dr. Jim Slater, was one of the top administrators at Loma Linda University.

Dr. James Slater was a radiation oncologist whose career was driven by the desire to improve cancer patients' quality of life. He was a highly respected man, a man of high moral and ethical character, and he was widely mourned when he died in January 2019. He had gained a reputation as "the pioneer of proton therapy" after spearheading the creation of the world's first hospital-based proton treatment center at Loma Linda University Health System, and served as the chair of the department of radiation medicine at the university for several decades.

Through my sister-in-law, Vanguard was able to get a meeting with Dr. Slater. We told him that we were comfortable with our shavers being tested and a study published. Our only request, made respectfully, was that a chain of custody be established. The cause for our concern was that Smith & Nephew had custody of the products prior to submitting them to the Loma Linda orthopedic department. We said we would gladly provide the products—or, if he preferred, he could send his representatives to our plant to randomly collect the devices. We also agreed to send the products to an independent lab for the testing, and to cover the related expenses. If the results were unfavorable, we would hold ourselves accountable.

Thanks to Dr. Slater's integrity and expertise, he recognized that in order to conduct a scientific study, a chain of custody was appropriate and scientifically sound. As a result, he immediately instructed the department to halt testing and cease all study-related work until a chain of custody could be established. For reasons I can't begin to fathom, the head of the orthopedic department tried to circumvent Dr. Slater's directive and continue with the study. Although Dr. Slater was a patient and soft-spoken man, his anger was kindled by this betrayal, and he confronted the individual in question. Dr. Slater assured this person that he had a choice: comply with Dr. Slater's order or look for other employment.

Smith & Nephew's tactic revealed just how much pain Vanguard was starting to cause the kingdom and how far its Big Dogs were willing to go to end it. These guys were, no pun intended, going to play dirty. Again and again, similar situations would arise. One can debate what or who was protecting us, but only a fool would debate the fact that we were being protected.

It didn't take long for the need for protection to become very apparent.

Chapter 10

No Man's Land

Fear is the absence of faith.

— Chuck Masek

We knew our devices worked, we knew they were clean, and we knew they were sterile. We also knew that there were Big Dogs barking loudly enough that they were impossible to ignore. They were focused on accusing us of essentially using a garden hose to clean off bloody instruments out back of the building. The question we had to ask ourselves was how we could drown out their yapping by using scientific evidence.

As providence would have it, the Big Dogs' message was that customers should go and see for themselves what we were doing in the plant. What they didn't take into account was that this would give Vanguard the platform to speak directly to doctors, nurses, and other decision-makers. The results from those plant tours became a game-changer for us. Our investment in ensuring that the facility had the same look and feel as a hospital provided visitors with a reassuring sense of familiarity and proved to be money well spent. I imagine the prevailing assumption in the kingdom was that when our processes were subjected to scrutiny, it would be made clear to everyone—even to us—that we had no business reprocessing SUDs.

But if visitors expected to see a jerry-rigged sailboat, what they found instead was a luxury yacht.

Alsobrook Street had never been set up for plant tours. Moving to Great Oak Drive allowed us to design and build a facility with plant tours specifically in mind. We invested in our flooring, making sure its gleam rivaled what was found in a hospital. We cut multiple windows in the plant's internal walls, through which production could be viewed. This signaled the transparency of our process. To further prove that we had nothing to hide, whoever led the plant tour—usually Dave McElhaney, Vanguard's vice president of sales—referenced a reprocessed arthroscopic shaver that was framed and hanging on the wall. This device was so trusted by Ellyn Bender, a Vanguard director who worked in the quality department, that she requested it be used instead of a new one during her own surgery.

The Big Dogs never realized that it wasn't worth it to us to reprocess even the most lucrative device if it couldn't be done safely. "What if it was your mom?" was the question that framed everything we did and, perhaps more importantly, *didn't* do.

Plant tours were expensive due to the cost of visitors' flights, hotel stays, and our time. Dave made a practice of taking our visitors out to dinner the night before, then join them for breakfast the morning of the tour. He spent so much time at the Terrace Hotel that he was given his own parking spot near the front door and was able to leave some of his belongings in a room during his rare breaks between back-to-back and even back-to-back-to-back plant tours.

The Big Dogs almost *dared* their customers to see for themselves what we were doing in the plant. What visitors found were people who were confident they were doing the right thing for the right reason and could communicate it in the right way. Even

Jeff, who was a trained accountant, would sometimes lead the tours. He had only entered the reprocessing industry because Bill Frisbey had asked him to do the due diligence ahead of our acquisition of Encore. With an authenticity that no scientist could dispute, Jeff would look at our gowned-up guests and proclaim, "At Vanguard, we are pioneering a brand-new industry."

When the Big Dogs realized that plant tours, though a financial strain on us, were not only helping us gain the support of potential customers but also giving us a voice, they knew they needed to shift strategy to a more external battlefield. The new front in their war? They hammered on the fact that although our devices were safe, we had no FDA clearance to market them. This clearance, known as a 510(k), is nothing more than a claim of substantial equivalence submitted to the FDA by a company that wants to bring a product to market. Essentially, it is a way for a company to claim "I'm just like them!"

Unfortunately for us, at that time the FDA wouldn't grant a 510(k) clearance to any reprocessor. Unlike manufacturers or specs developers, reprocessors were entities with which the agency had no experience. There literally existed no box on the submission form for us to check.

While we were stumbling through the regulatory wilderness, the Big Dogs kept hitting our current and prospective customers with the fact that we had no clearance. It didn't matter that our plant and processes looked good. We were regulated under the quality system regulations (QSR) in the same way as the OEMs, but the rallying cry throughout the Big Dog Kingdom was *No 510(k)s!*

As that conflict raged, the Big Dogs continued to assert that our devices were not clean—and, in fact, were contaminated with blood. We were in a regulatory no man's land. We couldn't get the

FDA to accept an application from us for a 510(k), and we were simultaneously being snarled at over the fact that we couldn't possibly prove our devices were clean—because we had no 510(k)s! It was regulatory purgatory.

Holding firm to our center, however, we set about to prove that our reprocessed devices were in fact cleaner than the new devices being marketed by the Big Dogs. Although we had to invest massive amounts of time and money to develop the data, we were able to scientifically validate that our reprocessed devices, tested by an outside laboratory, had less contamination than the manufacturers' new devices. Again, we won on science and caused another Big Dog battle tactic to fail.

Around 1998, one of the Big Dogs decided to revisit a tactic previously used by Smith & Nephew. Boston Scientific, our old foe, went into one of our hospitals and retrieved, literally off a shelf, approximately thirty GI biopsy forceps that we had reprocessed. They must have notified the FDA around the same time, as we were told that the FDA had gone into the same hospital and taken approximately twenty more GI biopsy forceps from the same lot. Vanguard went into the same hospital and retrieved the remaining biopsy forceps from that lot.

It was not surprising at all when Boston Scientific notified the FDA that they had tested the biopsy forceps and found 45 percent of them contaminated.

The FDA tested a few of the biopsy forceps they had collected—and found them sterile.

Next, we tested ours—and also found them sterile.

Boston Scientific asked the FDA to test the remaining forceps in their possession by cutting up the devices. They reasoned that doing so would ensure that every part of the device would be exposed to the testing broth. They were definitely reaching.

It wouldn't be the last time I was asked by the FDA to meet with them. This time, it was with Dr. Larry Kessler, who was the director of the FDA Office of Science and Technology. He explained what Boston Scientific wanted.

"Larry," I said, flabbergasted, "you're a scientist, just like me. You know that the more you manipulate a device before introducing it to the testing broth, the more opportunity exists that you might accidently contaminate the device, thus leading to a false positive."

The expression on Larry's face gave away nothing. This was, after all, a man who had cited "enforcement discretion" as the reason the FDA hadn't yet come after third-party reprocessors under the Big Dogs' rising pressure.

I continued, "More importantly, your department has established protocols in place for testing these devices. These protocols require that you place them in the testing broth without any manipulation." What I said next would either win or lose the argument. "Are you willing to violate your own protocols to accommodate a request from a manufacturer who has a vested interest in the outcome?"

I will never forget how he looked me straight in the eyes and said, "We will follow our written protocols."

Shortly thereafter, Larry notified Boston Scientific of his decision. We had won this battle. But from the Big Dogs' perspective, the war was far from over.

* * *

My partnership with Doug, and our first experience with the FDA, had occurred a few years before Vanguard existed, while we were both still at EnviroMed. The agency isn't big on providing advance warning that they'll be stopping by, so when an investigator, a woman named Reva, showed up unannounced, it wasn't entirely unexpected. She wore what looked like military whites—and a pronounced scowl.

I had no doubt that our products were clean and that our processes benefitted the environment. Her job was to ask questions—a lot of questions. From my perspective as a microbiologist, it was clear that Reva didn't understand the science behind my responses. It therefore didn't take long for her to get under my skin, and for me to get under hers. Doug heard us, shall I say, debating loudly, and it was clear to him that there was only one way this was going to go. He needed to step in and do something before we found ourselves shut down and locked out of the facility.

When the FDA inspects, there are two tracks they can take. They can look at a few major systems and, if they don't see anything that causes concern, swiftly leave. The second track, which, thanks to my attitude, we were already hurtling toward, was that they could stay for several days and comb through absolutely everything. Reva definitely saw something that bothered her—and that something was me. What had started off as a simple inspection turned into a three-day crucible.

Doug wasted no time pulling me out of the inspection process and pushing himself in, telling me to get lost if I wanted EnviroMed to survive it. Thanks to Doug taking over, we got off without even a warning letter. Reva gave Doug a copy of the federal regulations, suggesting that he might want to pass them along to me, since it was clear from my answers that I couldn't possibly have seen them before.

Some years later, at Vanguard, we requested and arranged for several high-level FDA personnel to tour the facility. This was not an inspection. We wanted to educate the FDA about our industry and how to regulate it. As it turned out, Reva's name was on the list of attendees. When I caught sight of it, I didn't take my chances that she wouldn't remember me—I once again made myself scarce.

What was evident from my limited but memorable interaction with the FDA was that although the scientific method would steer our processes, at some point interpretation would come into play. When it comes to dealing with the FDA, the burden is on you to prove that what you're doing is safe. The goal is to successfully defend your processes. We could win business thanks to the data we presented to potential customers. Steve's Magic software program could aggregate the data we needed from, for example, the sterilization process. We could develop a six- or seven-page report for the customer and eliminate any emotion-based bias they held toward reprocessing. But a single report wasn't going to cut it with the FDA.

We were definitely a "measure twice, cut once" kind of company. Getting slammed to the floor by the FDA over and over again was something we believed we could handle, even if we didn't realize how that kind of continuous pressure could wear an organization down. We knew how to extrapolate data, and because our processes were so stringent, we had no problem presenting our results. The problem came down to differences of opinion about those results.

Robin learned this the hard way during her first interaction with an FDA inspector. After listening to Robin's presentation, the inspector said, "I can tell from your body language that you're either incredibly nervous or you're lying to me."

None of us had gone to school or been trained on how to deal with the FDA. But we got a lot of practice keeping emotion out of our responses and managing our nonverbal signals, because we were inspected every year—*every single year*. That didn't happen in the industry. The Big Dogs thought they were unlucky if they saw an inspector once every five years. Vanguard, however, got a Notice of Adverse Findings (commonly referred to in the industry as a Form 483) every year. Doug would take a long look at the attached itemized list and tell me, "There's no way we're going to be able to make all of these corrections."

As a first step, we had thirty days to submit a reasonable plan to the FDA which included deadlines for resolution of all the issues they had noted. Until the next inspection, all company weapons had to be focused on those targets. Then the next inspection would come around and we'd be hammered all over again, albeit on new items. There was no doubt that the FDA saw Vanguard as a "target-rich environment."

After getting hit a few more times, we came to realize that we had to do more than just know the regulations and how to meet them; we had to understand statistics and have ways to capture data that wouldn't necessarily make sense to people who weren't scientists and who only had the regulations to guide them.

So, we set up experiments, which led to Seth discovering something that played a big part in his evolution as an industry professional. He would go to his college stats class and learn something, then come back to Vanguard and apply what he'd just learned to an analysis he and Doug were working on. These experiments needed to stand up to scientific scrutiny *and* be replicable, as the FDA was only interested in results that could be consistently proven. So much of Doug and Seth's time wasn't spent proving that the cleaning system worked—when it came to the FDA, we were more often than not proving that the cleaning system was valid.

After being asked about it over and over, we recognized that the core question the FDA wanted us to answer, using consistent data to support our response, was "Well, how do you know?" One inspector, a man named Kevin Vogel, whom Doug in particular came to know *very* well, may have been asking how we knew, for instance, that the temperature of the steam was high enough in a pressurized vessel. But what he was really asking was "How do you know it's high enough?" The only way to know that you'd answered the question to Kevin's satisfaction was when he stopped challenging you with another question about that rationale and moved on. What came of these questions, I see now, was that we learned to ask them of ourselves. We could think critically, ask, "How do you know?" and then prove things to ourselves when neither the FDA nor anyone else was looking.

The screws really started to tighten—for Doug, especially— when he found himself spending thirty days at a time sequestered in his office with Kevin, essentially justifying our existence. At the same time, I kept talking about a "wave of devices" and pushing him to work on new products. You don't come to have seventeen different product categories without doing a lot of testing. One day could easily see Doug working on electrophysiology (EP) catheters, only to turn around the next day and see him working on orthopedic burrs, bits, and blades. These were vastly different devices, operating according to wildly different principles. It could take weeks to test a new device, and there were more than a few times when we determined that reprocessing couldn't be done or wasn't worth it. While I was constantly stretching the limits of Doug's imagination, I also stretched the limits of his patience by continually telling him, no matter the device in question, "It's a no-brainer." Doug says I seemed to believe every device was a no-brainer.

The routine went something like this. I'd run into Doug's office all excited about some new medical device, such as an EP catheter, and ask him, "Hey, can you do this?" Because he didn't want to dampen my excitement, and got a lot of personal enjoyment out of testing products, we worked hard to expand new lines, while simultaneously trying to keep existing ones on the market by keeping the FDA off our backs.

We would set up the procedures knowing that Kevin was going to beat us up as badly as he could. It changed the way we approached the work. We recognized that we needed to operate in such a way that we could answer any criticisms that arose. It might have looked like our protocols were unnecessarily strict, or that we were spending a lot of money in support of internal R&D testing that wasn't required, but this investment brought us peace of mind and helped steel us for the onslaught when Kevin showed up for one of his thirty-day stints at Vanguard.

Dealing with the FDA certainly reinforced the notion that you can't inspect quality into a process. But it wasn't because of the agency that we built quality into our processes—we had done so from day one, whether anyone was watching or not, because it was the right thing to do.

Part III

The War Rages On

Cry "Havoc!" and let slip the dogs of war.
—William Shakespeare, *Julius Caesar*

CHAPTER 11

THE FEAR AND DOUBT CAMPAIGN

Facts are stubborn things.

— Vern Feltner

The Big Dogs had been sniffing around us for some time when we made the decision to start reprocessing GI biopsy forceps. With this move—one they viewed as a clear provocation—we became more than a nuisance to them. We became the enemy.

Our encroachment on their domain quickly made it evident to the Big Dogs that their power alone wouldn't be enough to defeat us. Vanguard was many times smaller and far weaker, but we were also nimble in a way they weren't. They hadn't had to be for quite some time. From the shaded comfort of their porch, they merely had to keep one watchful eye open because, prior to our intrusion, no one had dared come close to their fence. So, whereas their control of the SUD reprocessing industry had long been absolute, they had only recently discovered that we were hungry strays who wouldn't be satisfied with scraps.

Their knee-jerk reaction of lowering prices on the forceps instead of raising them, thus safeguarding their revenue, was a disastrous misstep right out of the gate. Strategy can be adjusted, but an expeditious victory is always preferable. This emotion-fueled decision left the Big Dogs frenzied, and we certainly weren't yet in a position to advance on them. We were therefore fortunate that we didn't *have* to. Their decision to lower prices resulted in a massive boost in our business and the cannibalization of their own, which allowed us to build up some much-needed reserves while theirs drained just a little.

We knew that our already aggressive challenger would be antagonized into action, the more so because they only had themselves to blame for the drying up of the GI biopsy forceps revenue stream. Their posturing had, until this point, been a daunting challenge for us to outmaneuver. Their impending declaration of war offered no possibility of fending them off or enabling a quiet retreat. Our rebel days were over. There could be no avoiding it—we were going to have to face them on the battlefield.

The days of the Big Dogs allowing their hatred to drive their assaults against us were over. This war, as far as they were concerned, would be won or lost on strategy. Brute force had gotten them nowhere; they would rely on their deep and lengthy experience in an industry where they believed we didn't belong.

Health care costs were continuing to rise, and Vanguard had proven we could achieve the same *or better* cleaning outcomes than the hospitals' central processing departments at a significantly lower cost. Vanguard guaranteed the sterility of the devices while shouldering all the liability. Customers were starting to think we couldn't be *that* bad.

The Big Dogs knew they needed to head us off at the pass and leverage customers' immediate "yuck-factor" responses before common sense and logic revealed the truth about SUD reprocessing. The Big Dogs thought that *if* decision-makers saw for themselves the yuck factor in what they portrayed to our customer as our inferior cleaning systems, surely that would keep the customer loyal to the Big Dogs—misinformed, but loyal. The fact that Vanguard would pay the costs of losing potential business was a bonus.

But the reaction they anticipated from customers never materialized, and soon our impressed potential customers became satisfied ongoing customers. And it wasn't simply because the economics of health care left them little choice.

Contrary to expectations, opening our plant's doors for face-to-face examination enabled Vanguard to win over even the most reticent customers, because their own eyes didn't lie to them. Neither did the numbers. For example, take the projected savings from compression sleeves, which were used on surgical patients to keep their blood flowing. The sleeves were typically discarded after the patient was released. The savings from reprocessing this single category of device ranged from $90,000 a year for one fair-size hospital to tens of millions of dollars a year for a large network of hospitals. When it came to devices costing several thousand dollars apiece, the savings skyrocketed.

As hospitals started to make the shift toward SUD reprocessing and actively defended it, the Big Dogs' mission shifted to finding a new weakness to exploit. Vanguard's lack of regulatory clearance was just the perceived weakness they were looking for. With a rallying howl of "No 510(k)s!" the Big Dogs moved to the regulatory battlefield. Vanguard's counter tactic was to educate our customers about how we already operated under the same QSR (the FDA's Quality System Regulations) as the manufacturers.

There were no FDA requirements about the number of times a device could be used. Vanguard invested in policies and procedures that required each device to be marked with a unique identifying number that enabled us to keep records of the history of the device, to include all of the reprocessing steps taken for that device, the collection site, the job control number, and the number of times the device had been reprocessed. Tracking this data, we knew the precise number of times a device could safely be reprocessed. Just as a product was rejected if it failed quality checks at any point, it couldn't be reprocessed beyond the maximum number of times deemed safe. In this way, we covered the bases of sterility *and* safe functionality.

So, their FDA clearance argument failed to leave any bite marks on us. The Big Dogs' next move was to wound us where we were strongest, so that the damage would spread to our weaker parts. They tried to turn our greatest weapon, the undisputed science, against us. They asserted to our customers that our devices weren't clean. As they knew and we knew, if a device cannot be cleaned, it cannot possibly be guaranteed to be sterile.

What the Big Dogs didn't account for was that we could scientifically prove that not only were our devices clean, they actually had less contaminates on them than *new* devices. They may have cited, ad nauseam, the few studies documenting patients who had been treated and gone on to develop infections, but they strangely failed to mention that the devices used on those patients were brand new. Unlike the OEMs, we inspected *every single device.*

The kingdom was unwilling to cede any territory to us, even if their tactics to date had resulted in Vanguard sales increasing. By 2000, we were reprocessing more than a million devices a year. We boasted more than eight hundred hospital customers and employed more than four hundred people, all while operating out of 125,000 square feet.

It took this kind of maturation for the Big Dogs to realize that their victory would never lie with the customer. After running directly into that fence over and over, they finally took stock of their injuries and recognized that any chance of defeating us would have to come from the FDA. If the Big Dogs couldn't convince customers that what we were doing was unclean and unsafe, they would howl at the only entity that could.

Until the mid-nineties, the FDA hadn't paid much attention to the reprocessing of SUDs. They were well aware that although medical device makers advised strongly against it, hospitals had long been cleaning and sterilizing devices in-house before reusing them. This kind of hospital reprocessing avoided federal and industry oversight, since the devices were an integral part of the facilities' cost-cutting efforts, were not being sold externally, and were part of a heavily self-governed practice. People at the FDA had long been confident in the controls of hospitals. If reprocessing was occurring, it was at least being safely managed. Also, the devices' original manufacturers were required to submit 510(k)s, so initial oversight was seen as having been achieved. From the point that hospitals purchased devices, the liability for function, safety, and quality became theirs, and they had too much to lose by not following safe and effective practices.

It was only when Larry Spears, director of the enforcement division of the FDA, attended a public conference centered on reprocessing reusable devices that questions unexpectedly started to come at him like rapid fire:

Are they clean?

How can this possibly be safe?

Why isn't the FDA doing anything about it?

How the hell can this even be legal?

With this barrage of concern and curiosity, Larry came to realize that the conversation around reprocessing SUDs was only going to get louder and more heated.

Although SUD reprocessing would become as much of a struggle within the FDA as it was in the marketplace, the practice initially seemed to many in the agency like mere whining from the Big Dogs.

Why are you letting them work on this stuff?

They can't be doing this!

What are you going to do about it?

These were questions that for some time would have no answer. The FDA was in desperate need of more information, because only when they understood more about the practice could they determine what, if anything, they were going to do about it. Getting involved was a big step for the agency. Just because the Big Dogs were passionate about getting the FDA involved didn't mean that there was enough justification to move forward. Scrutinizing reprocessing could either become a feather in the agency's cap or else draw it into complicity in killing off a legitimate practice for financial reasons that clearly benefitted one side.

Questions about patient safety continued to nudge the FDA toward finding some answers. There was a war being fought in the marketplace and within the agency, with some internal activists and scientists calling for regulation. Pursuing regulation of SUD reprocessing was considered a major move. Medical device manufacturers waged a media campaign to publicize the practice and force the agency's hand, but the FDA thankfully refused to be swayed by those who had the loudest bark. The agency's first step was to pierce the fog of war and gather verifiable information. For that, they needed participants willing to turn over their data—a lot of data.

* * *

Vanguard's desire to assist the FDA was really as simple as recognizing that reprocessing SUDs was the right thing to do. By trusting the science, we could provide evidence for the financial, safety, and ecological reasons why SUD reprocessing should be sanctioned at the highest levels of agency oversight. Even on an uneven battlefield, outmatched and outnumbered by dogs slavering to tear across the field, this was the strategy that had always protected us. The medical device market was worth approximately $60 billion a year—why would we *not* want to reveal our processes to the people who could legitimize us and end the war once and for all? Fighting for so long had taken a toll, so if a nod from the FDA could help us and the other third-party reprocessors to take a bigger bite out of the market and end the pain, well, why not? How hard could it be?

For Vanguard's quality assurance department, however, the ongoing and unrelenting presence of an FDA inspector represented the greatest challenge of Doug's career. According to Larry Spears, Vanguard was viewed by the agency as the most visible and viable independent reprocessor, and therefore was the natural supplier of the information the FDA required.

The first step was taken within the agency, as they needed to determine whether regulation was required and whether they were the most appropriate government entity to provide it. It seemed to make sense that, since they were already regulating the OEMs, it should also fall on them to regulate the reprocessors. Individuals and groups within the agency who were in favor of regulation were asking, "Why not?" Those who were opposed were trying to find reasons why it was a bad idea.

The FDA knew where the Big Dogs stood. Reprocessors were digging into their profits, and they didn't want the practice to continue. They yapped about patient safety, which of course left providers and their patients in the crosshairs. Inaction by the FDA could potentially lead to collateral damage to the public it was charged with protecting, so there was no real choice for them but to take action.

The first question the FDA wanted answered was how great a risk was posed to the public by what we were doing. Reported infections from our devices would have been one thing, but that was not what had drawn the agency's attention. Vague concern spurred by the Big Dogs led to increased curiosity. As a result, more people within the FDA became ready to explore the possibility of regulation. Larry Spears's vision was that the FDA could play a critical role in an American success story.

Vanguard answered every question the FDA asked. It felt to Doug like being killed over and over again, as he personally took most of the bullets. But due to his hard work, the agency came to realize that they had fully rebutted the "Why not?" questions. The FDA followed the data to separate those companies that were serious from those that were only looking to make a quick buck. The companies that survived regulation deserved to stay in and help to grow the industry; those that couldn't withstand the requirements that came with oversight deserved to be forced out of the pack.

FDA inspections even reached the hospitals. Their reactions to scrutiny of a practice they had been doing unimpeded for years were, to put it mildly, mixed. Noncompliance with proper disinfection and sterilization practices was a growing problem; as a result, reprocessing in many hospitals was shut down. If you ask Larry Spears, who no longer works in the government sector, his view is that the FDA's involvement was a good thing for this very reason.

The agency also very much appreciated Vanguard's help, according to Larry—and it *was* considered help, because although the FDA quickly understood that regulation was required and that they were the ones who should do it, they didn't know *how* to do it. Thanks to our willingness to take the hits, safety across the entire SUD reprocessing industry was improved.

Thanks to the standards Vanguard already held itself to and was then forced to demonstrate under scrutiny, we became even better. We became more adept at planning and carrying out testing in a way that would stand up to rigorous questioning, and we became skilled at researching and writing with a degree of elegance about the evidentiary findings in support of our data.

We weren't only creative in how we captured the data. We were also committed. Many nights were spent at the plant writing policy or procedures that would allow us to see the logical stream of regulation and how, if properly applied, it would result in improvements. Doug in particular pulled quite a few all-nighters; it wasn't at all unusual to find him asleep in his office the next morning after not going home the night before.

We knew we had the data to support our customers. We designed with intricacy and detail to get the big picture right—a picture that depicted a sophisticated process comprised of automated cleaning systems that functioned without the complicating factor of human involvement.

Despite having specialists in every category of device, the FDA hadn't known how to treat us. When it became clear that our processes—and indeed our very existence—were based on the same facts and overwhelming scientific data that the agency abided by, we became partners.

CHAPTER 12

FRIENDLY FIRE

The saddest thing about betrayal is that it never comes from your enemies.

— Anonymous

When the Big Dogs finally came to realize that the FDA's attention was in fact welcomed by us—that we *wanted* the validation that regulation brought— they switched to a different strategy. They formed CARA, the Coalition Against Reuse Abuse. This was perhaps their weakest tactic, as the coalition went nowhere at all. Our company remained unified and unyielding against the pressure. However, as often happens in a prolonged war, a few people faltered, and the first cracks in our armor began to show.

Kerry Hicks joined the company in 1993 and became our sales representative in South Carolina. Sometime later, he was appointed the national sales manager, working with the reps we already had and helping to find new ones. Marge, ever astute, was always bothered by the fact that when Kerry typed the name of the company, he would put the "a" before the "u," as in "Vangaurd." I tried to correct him several times, since he was essentially selling Vanguard and its vision to new reps, but Kerry didn't take my advice.

Although Mark had come to the company with an extensive background in sales, for a time he reported to Kerry. Mark would sometimes call me and say, "Chuck, I just spoke to Kerry Hicks. I think he was still in his pajamas—at ten o'clock in the morning." Or, after a meeting with Kerry, Mark might shake his head and acknowledge that Kerry had been asking some embarrassingly basic questions about how to manage a national sales force. It became very clear that Kerry Hicks was not the best person for the job. Even more disconcerting was the evidence that he and Bill Stover—our rep in Arkansas, and the man who had brought EP catheters to Vanguard—were making plans to compete with our company. Before Bill flew down to Florida to meet with me, I already had the sense that he wanted to be more than a rep.

One day he, Bill Frisbey, and I were in my office and Stover started making demands about what he wanted from the company: a larger percentage of ownership, more commission, and other demands that were hard to swallow. I have always liked to see others prosper, but Stover's litany of demands went on and on, and it became obvious that he was shaking down the company.

Nevertheless, I acquiesced to everything he asked for, and was more than fair. Toward the end of the conversation, he turned to me with one more demand. To this day, I can't remember what it was he wanted, although I do recall it being something insignificant. Though that final demand was minor, my response wasn't. Something inside me snapped.

I looked Stover directly in the eyes and said, "We're done here. No deal."

Stover got back on the plane and flew home to Arkansas with nothing. Then he enlisted Kerry Hicks, and together they decided to form Paragon Healthcare. Paragon ultimately didn't have much under the hood—the eventual modest sale price to another company attested to this—but Kerry and Bill were successful at taking away (or, as some employees viewed it, stealing) much of Vanguard's EP catheter business.

Even Bill Frisbey, who had been my sales trainer at Travenol and who'd saved Vanguard from one of its many threats by helping us secure investment, would eventually be swayed by Paragon's apparent early success. Because the war was raging so violently outside Vanguard, I wasn't as attuned as I should have been to the internal threats we were facing. Seth has another theory. Maybe one of my greatest strengths, my loyalty, led to me trusting others too much, and often to my own detriment. Any strength taken to an extreme can become a weakness.

When Doug and Mark mentioned to me privately that they were concerned about Bill Frisbey, I respected their apprehension, yet I failed to act. After all, there was nothing specific to act on at the time. As a matter of fact, Bill didn't have the necessary shares to do anything detrimental to the company, though he definitely tried. Instead of going after Vanguard, he decided to come after me.

Perhaps he was unable to deal with how the tables had turned, and that he was now reporting to me, or he may have believed that he knew a better way to run the company. Whatever his motivation, at a shareholders' meeting he unexpectedly called for a vote to remove me as CEO.

It was a strange and reckless thing to do, and I still don't fully understand why he did it. He went after me *knowing* he didn't have the shares or the votes of other shareholders necessary to succeed. My relationship with him spanned a few companies and several decades. But the deed was done, and I wasted no time in firing him.

What was worse, he was belligerent about the situation, so I firmly informed him that he wouldn't be getting a severance. Bill wasn't able to harm me—he couldn't—but I ultimately did pay out a hefty severance anyway. I didn't want to be a slave to anger or vengeance, so I made a place in my heart for forgiveness. At a time when several other battles were raging, it wasn't a smart move to add another one.

Then, in June 2000, we had no choice but to get involved in another skirmish that led to firing another of our salesmen. He had given his password for the Vanguard internal website to our competitor, Alliance Medical.

Alliance was tracking Vanguard's sales closely. They had invested more than twice as much money as we had yet were only keeping pace with our growth. I never let go of the idea that the goal was to eventually sell Vanguard. In order to do that, we made no apology for continuing to run lean. It wasn't just that Alliance's management methodology differed from ours. They prioritized profit above all else, which led to some very questionable practices. What they did with that "stolen" website password was unquestionably wrong, so we sued them to prove it.

One of Nathan's daily activities—he was seventeen years old and at that time working summers in our IT department—was to look at the logs for the website in order to monitor usage. Sales reps could log in to build a sales order and check their individual sales, usage, and customer reports—important information that in the hands of anyone outside of Vanguard could prove very valuable. So, we checked the logs daily to make sure that reps were accessing the information so we could stay ahead of any issues that might arise.

Nathan saw five to ten hits per rep on an average day. On one day, though, he noticed several *hundred* hits, all coming from one area in Arizona.

"Do we have a rep in Phoenix?" he asked Steve.

Steve answered, "We don't have a sales rep in Phoenix—but our biggest competitor is based out there."

It didn't take Nathan long to put two and two together. He went back to his computer, then yelled, "Steve!" Those several hundred hits had already increased to over a thousand, and were continuing to rise.

Steve, now looking over Nathan's shoulder at the frenetic activity, cried out, "Shut it down! Shut the website down!"

Alliance had downloaded almost every single document on our sales portal.

We initiated legal proceedings against Alliance. Over the next few months, the lawsuit progressed slowly. The timing couldn't have been worse, as our war with the Big Dogs was nearing critical mass. We had no choice but to hit back and ensure that what we'd worked so hard to build wasn't swiped by a company that should have been an ally.

* * *

It wasn't just within Vanguard that things took an ominous turn. I'll never forget when we were out in Phoenix with our lawyers for the deposition of Rick Ferreira, an upper-level executive at Alliance. As I was trying to gear up for what promised to be a grueling day, my cell phone rang. It was six o'clock on the morning of September 11, 2001, and I wondered through the fog of half-sleep who could possibly be calling me so early in the day.

As I answered the call, I realized it was Marge on the other end. She wouldn't ordinarily want to disturb me at such an hour, so I knew something must be up. "Marge?" I asked by way of a greeting, perhaps subconsciously aware that this would be no ordinary conversation.

"They're dead," she said.

"What? Who's dead?" I somewhat groggily asked. "Who's dead, Marge?"

"They're all dead…"

I was awake now. "Is it the dog, Marge?"

"They're all dead…"

"The children?" I felt my stomach drop and my knees begin to weaken. *Oh God, no.*

She told me to turn on the television, and when I did, I saw the second plane traveling across it, head-on into the second tower.

"Stay calm, Marge," I said, feeling relief at the thought of my children's safety and then instantly guilt for such a reaction. "I'll be right back with you, honey."

I dialed Seth and told him to stay with his mother until I got home.

The deposition was all but forgotten. During moments like these one is reminded of what's really important, so I wasted no time in calling my travel agent, who advised me that the best way to get back to Florida would be to rent a car and drive. I'd have to do it as soon as possible, he warned, since cars were being snapped up by other people hurrying home to their loved ones.

When you're twenty years old, a road trip with your friends is a good time. When you're fifty and have two lawyers along for the three-day ride, it's not quite as much fun. When we crossed the

Florida state line, though, it was the most beautiful feeling—and I know the lawyers felt it, too. *Home.*

We had another eight hours from Pensacola to Tampa. I remember spending some of those hours thinking about how Marge's first response had been to cry and grieve for the innocent people who'd died, and for their loved ones whose lives would be changed forever. Although I felt deep sorrow for all these victims, my first response had been that we needed to hunt down the people responsible for this cowardly act.

* * *

The litigation with Alliance was eventually settled through mediation. Their original offer for the breach of our website was $15,000, but they ultimately agreed to pay us $200,000. Little did either side know that we weren't through with each other—not by a long shot.

CHAPTER 13

POLITICAL ANIMALS

All politics are local.

— Tip O'Neill

Y ears before, when we were a new start-up, *Forbes* magazine had introduced us to their readers in an article entitled "Blood Money." The title of the article made my blood run cold as I considered the possible damaging implications for Vanguard. But, taken as a whole, it was generally positive.

A follow-up piece, published in 2001, described us as a company whose best friend was—surprise!—the FDA. About me the article claimed, "It is the rare entrepreneur who begs for government control." What wasn't included in this short piece was any mention of the number of years we had already been asking, almost begging, for governmental regulation. The new article was published under the unfortunate and off-putting title, "Used Catheters for Sale." Not the message we were hoping to send.

Several years before the first article was published, Mark and I had requested a meeting with FDA officials. The plan was to fly up to DC and request regulation from those few agency employees who were willing to meet with us in person.

In any meeting, it's easy to spot who is in upper-level management by where they are seated. The more important you are, the closer to the action you'll sit—usually in the middle of the conference table. For our meeting with the FDA, to our surprise, we entered the room and discovered three rings of chairs and twenty or more people surrounding the table. Seated in the center, flanking Mark and me, were the top ten employees at the agency. To say the situation was intimidating would be a significant understatement.

It was evident from the number of people present that the FDA had a real interest in meeting with us and learning more about Vanguard and the reprocessing of SUDs. Up to this point, only the howling Big Dogs had been in the agency's ear, so I didn't beat around the bush. "We know you're aware of what's going on," I said. "And that there are other companies telling you we're putting patients at risk. This is *not* true!"

We were aware that it wasn't enough for us to be as good as any Big Dog; we had to be better. "Tell us what you want us to do, and we'll do it," I said, confident that we could meet even their highest requirements. We knew we weren't putting patients at risk, and all we wanted was the chance to prove it publicly.

The agency recommended that we get with the other reprocessors, our competition, and form a trade association to represent our interests in the same way the Medical Device Manufacturers Association (MDMA) represented the manufacturers. This meant that in the next phase of our war with the Big Dog Kingdom, the independent reprocessors would need to be fighting side by side. As a united front, we would promote legitimization and a conclusion to the war that had already dispatched many of us and remained an ever-present threat to those of us who were still standing.

At the end of 1997 we formed the Association of Medical Device Reprocessors (AMDR), a trade association for third-party reprocessors of single-use medical devices. AMDR is based in Washington, DC, so over the course of the next year, Mark would leave for DC on Sunday night and return on Saturday morning. Largely as a result of his full-time effort there, DC became the city where a deal would eventually be brokered and an armistice signed.

When AMDR was first formed, it included only three companies: Alliance, Vanguard, and SterilMed. From our point of view, suing Alliance wasn't a barrier to working alongside them—after all, business is business. These three companies accounted for approximately ninety percent of SUD reprocessing being done. Although Vanguard was the clear leader in the industry, as true brothers-in-arms, each company paid an equal one-third of the expenses related to AMDR. It was an expense that Vanguard couldn't really afford, but we also knew we couldn't afford *not* to invest in reinforcement that could sustain us if the war persisted.

Swiftly, AMDR became an incredible group of great minds focused on a shared victory. Bill Stoermer in particular brought a great deal to the table, thanks to his expertise and years of experience working for OEMs and hospitals. At that point he was the executive vice president of Alliance Medical Corporation.

Then and now, AMDR's responsibility is to align the medical device industry with the interests of hospitals and health care providers, and to continuously increase quality, reduce costs, and improve patient care.

Dan Vukelich, the current president and CEO of AMDR, says that the first time he met me, I said something along the lines of "Don't get too comfortable, kid—it's just a matter of time before Johnson &Johnson buys us out." A native of Minneapolis, Dan had stayed in DC after earning his political science degree at American University, and came to AMDR in 2000 after working on a political campaign. He had a law degree, which helped with the numerous legal, regulatory, and political issues that would soon propagate all along the SUDs reprocessing warfront.

If the FDA hadn't already received enough complaints about SUD reprocessing from the very vocal Big Dogs, the call that the agency received one Monday morning proved unavoidably incendiary. Despite our open appeal to the FDA to treat us the same as they did the Big Dogs, the practice of SUD reprocessing was still being hyped as secretive and hidden from the public. For Vanguard, that phone call, from the state of Illinois, set into motion another stage in the evolution of the ever-expanding war.

Even the most loyal and well-trained soldier can only fight for so long before fatigue sets in. Although I had always been able to shrug it off, I could feel it creep up on me even before the legislative front was opened. We were about to be rocked by a running gun battle across the country that would lock us in combat one state at a time.

It was on a Sunday afternoon when Illinois State Senator Evelyn Bowles (D–56th District) first heard about SUD reprocessing. An Associated Press article in the *St. Louis Post-Dispatch* was short on facts but long on emotion, and it had an immediate impact on her. Being in the position to do something about it, Senator Bowles made a call to the FDA the next day. She found that the people she spoke to had no information to share with her. Resolving to find some answers herself, she started her own investigation.

Shortly after the *St. Louis Post-Dispatch* article was published, we were in New Orleans at a North American Society for

Pacing and Electrophysiology (NASPE) conference. Marge and I hosted cocktails on a restaurant patio in the French Quarter. Mark, and regional managers Bryan Eckard, Mike Rovnak, Scott Wait, Mary Vermillon, and Mike Mayry were present and participating in the relaxation and fair amount of back-patting.

Scott Wait, our regional manager in St. Louis, Missouri, was typically calm and collected under fire, a man with a steady speaking voice. On this night, however, amid the casual banter, Scott's voice signaled definite alarm when he rushed out onto the balcony and declared, "Apparently, an Illinois state senator read an article in the St. Louis paper about reprocessing, and the reporter made claims that reprocessing is dangerous."

This got our attention. What Scott said next silenced all conversation. "Senator Bowles has filed a bill in the Illinois State Senate. It's basically a cut-and-paste of the article. But it's on its second reading." Although I didn't know it at the time, in the state of Illinois, a bill becomes law after the third reading. We had only one more reading to go.

A visibly panicked Scott concluded, "This is a fragile business."

With a questioning look on her face, Marge immediately turned to me. Her eyes gripping mine, she asked, "Fragile?"

Marge and I were well on our way to recovering from my fall, finally enjoying some financial freedom. I had a wife who deserved not to worry about losing everything and having to start over—yet again.

"He didn't mean *fragile*, honey," I said, guiding Marge away from the group and shooting daggers in Scott's direction. "He meant the business is … the business is fine."

Though we spent the rest of the evening focusing on the company's accomplishments, of which there were many, I knew Marge was still worried. I told her, with all the positivity I could muster, "Besides, honey, it's only one state." After a long pause, and with over-the-top optimism that gave away my own feeling of unease, I added, "There's another forty-nine left."

The next day, on the trade show floor, Mike Mayry was doing some glaring of his own as he walked past the Paragon booth. Instead of getting a few dirty looks back from our archrivals, Mike was surprised to see Bill Stover come out from behind the table. He was even more surprised when Stover unexpectedly slung an arm around his shoulders. The weight of Stover's arm was so bizarre, Mike remembers thinking, *What's about to happen here?* It didn't take long for him to find out.

"Did you hear," Stover said, his tone making clear that he believed he was relaying news, "that there's been legislation introduced in Illinois that would make what we do illegal?"

Mike had been present the night before when Scott used the word *fragile*, so he was among the first in the industry to learn about the legislation. Scott had learned the whole story from one of our reps, who had walked into a surgery center in Illinois to make a sale, only to be tossed a newspaper and a question: "Have you seen this?"

So, Mike knew about the bill, and now he knew that our competition also knew about the bill. After shrugging Stover's arm off his shoulder, Mike forced himself to walk over to me on the display floor. He caught my eye and wasted no time in turning his back and lowering his voice to tell me, "Paragon knows."

I processed instantly that this wasn't just a threat to Vanguard—this was a threat to the entire industry. The FDA could make us jump over a lot of hurdles, but we all knew that there was a light at the end of that bureaucratic tunnel. Legislation at the state level? Anything could be written into law—and if we didn't act immediately, it would be.

The industry was under assault. If we hoped to fight for the Vanguard slice of the pie, we first had to save the industry. I looked purposefully over at the Paragon booth and Bill Stover, and then I made my way over.

I imagine that the conversation between us must have looked animated to anyone watching, and Mike no doubt wondered what was being said, but within days everyone saw Vanguard and its archrivals as a united AMDR front, trying to protect our shared livelihood.

CHAPTER 14

A HERO RISES

Giants bleed like everybody else.

— Dan Groat

It wasn't just the Big Dogs and the FDA who recognized that what Vanguard was doing represented the future. A man by the name of Joseph Damico was also aware of how reprocessing SUDs was changing the dynamics and economics of the entire medical devices industry.

Joe had started out at American Hospital Supply (AHS) as a territory rep around the same time I was starting out at Baxter Travenol. Whereas I went the entrepreneurial route, Joe worked his way up the management ladder and became a very astute and well-regarded businessman. AHS was purchased by Baxter Travenol and then spun off a few years later because Wall Street never warmed up to the merger, which is how Allegiance was created. Allegiance was essentially the old AHS, and Joe served as president and CEO. In 1999, Allegiance was sold to Cardinal Healthcare. During his time as executive vice president at Cardinal, Joe became interested in the business of reprocessing SUDs, and thus in what Vanguard, as the industry-leading firm, was doing. Joe was, in fact, so interested that he approached the Cardinal people with the idea of buying Vanguard. Unfortunately, the other senior executives didn't find reprocessing as "neat" as Joe did.

When Cardinal bought Allegiance, one of the terms of the deal was that Joe would stay on at Cardinal for two years. And he did—two years to the day. Cardinal's decision not to acquire Vanguard cemented Joe's determination that he would leave, but he made that determination when he was only in year one of his two-year tenure. So, he had to wait.

* * *

The 1991 AORN conference in Atlanta had been the site of one of my lowest personal moments. However, while attending the 1997 AORN conference in Anaheim California, I met Joe for the first time. Joe simply walked up to the Vanguard booth, introduced himself, and asked me a few questions. It was clear he had an interest in the business, and I recall him mentioning that we should talk again soon.

During our short conversation I realized he had the ability to take Vanguard, and indeed the industry, to heights I could never have imagined. I would have considered myself a fool to dream of what would eventually come to pass. Joe, however, says he realized quickly that I had the ideas and approach of a true entrepreneur. He also understood that my ideas and approach were supported by more than enthusiasm. I wasn't using pseudoscience—I was practicing science.

* * *

Two years later at the 1999 AORN conference in San Francisco I met Joe again. By then, he had departed from Cardinal and started RoundTable Healthcare Partners, a private equity firm focused on the health care industry. His founding partners included Lester Knight, Jack McGinley, and Todd Warnock. Joe and his partners had decades of experience in managing, acquiring, and financing diversified health care companies, and were very interested in the pharmaceutical, consumer health, and medical device spaces.

Private equity firms raise money from wealthy individuals and institutions and invest in growing businesses. As of this writing, RoundTable has raised approximately $2.75 billion in committed capital. Their goal is to invest in small growing companies, then sell their stake in those companies at a later time for a significant profit, which would then be shared with their investors. Typically, the cycle of raising cash, buying into the businesses, and selling them takes five to seven years. Anything beyond this time frame is less than optimal because it adds to operating costs, and investors also grow anxious about realizing a return on their investment. After RoundTable raised its first fund, approximately half a billion dollars, they started to make their first round of investments. Joe was ready to make his move. At the top of his list was Vanguard.

I flew to Lake Forest, Illinois, where RoundTable was based, to discuss their acquisition of a majority interest in Vanguard. Things were looking good, and I was confident that we could reach a deal capable of bolstering us as we fought the Big Dogs. With RoundTable's fortifications, we could dare to dream. For the first time, we could know for certain that we would live to see the next day, and the day after that—a day that might include regulation. We knew for a fact that regulation was going to be costly. Investment from RoundTable could sustain us throughout the process and beyond, culminating in the lucrative sale of the company.

It was only when I was in the RoundTable offices and looked at their prospectus that I realized there might be a problem with the entire proposition. As I read through the guidelines that target companies had to align with to be considered by RoundTable, my stomach dropped. Vanguard didn't meet any of the guidelines. Not one! We weren't even close.

I was nervous. Feeling as I did, there was no way I would put Marge through this uncertainty. Even though I feared his answer, I had no choice but to ask, "Joe, is this something I should be concerned about?"

Joe said, "Don't worry about it, Chuck."

He didn't have to tell me twice. It was clear that Joe was emotionally invested in Vanguard. He liked the market space we were in so much that he was willing to circumvent RoundTable's own guidelines to be a part of it. Good enough for me!

This wasn't the last time the deal would be called into question. The original signing with RoundTable was scheduled for September 17, 2001. The plan had been for me to fly out to Phoenix for the Alliance deposition, stop in Florida, then fly to Illinois the next week to get the deal done. Everything changed with the 9/11 attacks.

The entire nation was blindsided. I had certainly never imagined that this enemy could come along and deliver such a blow to Vanguard. It was like receiving a sucker-punch—to be so close to the deal that would secure the future of the company, only to have it potentially snatched right out of my hands. It brought me to my knees. After everything we'd survived, for so many years and from so many opponents, losing the deal at that stage and in that way ushered in an unwelcome feeling: fear. I was genuinely afraid.

Nothing was functioning as it had before that devastating morning. I knew nothing would ever be the same again, and I knew I had to call Joe. I didn't want to, but my angst over not knowing what was happening with the deal was even stronger than the suffocating dread that told me it was all over. My grief hung heavy when I picked up the phone.

I wanted Joe to say that there was no need to wait, that we would still sign the documents in just a few days, but I knew this might no longer be possible. I was almost sick to my stomach with worry when I said to him, "I guess the deal's off."

We're done now was running through my head. *We're done now* was so loud in my mind that I wasn't entirely sure I'd heard Joe's reply. "Of course the deal's not off, Chuck. We're just going to push it out a week."

I could almost taste my relief. *Thank you, God.*

* * *

On September 24, 2001, RoundTable acquired a majority interest in Vanguard, putting an initial $12 million into the company. According to Joe, RoundTable's initial investment in Vanguard was driven by their belief that the reprocessing of medical devices would produce significant cost savings for hospitals and divert thousands of pounds of biomedical waste from landfills.

RoundTable has gone on to make more than forty investments and has never lost a single penny of investor money. But Joe admits that he underestimated the strong negative reaction that the acquisition of Vanguard brought—from everybody, it seemed. He wondered how it was possible that a company doing only $10 million in annual sales could be such a threat to the Big Dogs and their kingdom.

Very quickly, he came to appreciate that the negative reaction wasn't such a bad thing. Joe determined that we should embrace it and become *more* of a thorn in the Big Dogs' sides. That way, if they wanted the pain to stop, they would have to take us out. Injuring us had never served them well. Joe knew that with RoundTable in our corner the only way they could end their own misery was to buy us out.

Vanguard was the leader in its industry, which had made us an appealing acquisition for Joe and RoundTable. But it was a small industry. The real question that RoundTable faced was whether they believed they could help us. A good deal wasn't enough to get them involved; they had to know we would provide value to our customers and a strong return to the first investors in RoundTable.

Looking back, Joe considers that there was some naivete on everyone's part. He and his partners were convinced that SUD reprocessing had a permanent home in the health care industry. It wasn't a passing fad or shiny new object to throw money at. Joe admits, maybe they were either arrogant enough or cocky enough or dumb enough to believe that this was going to work.

That's not to say that our daily work at Vanguard became any less difficult when RoundTable came on board. It didn't. If anything, the dynamic shifted in such a way that we faced a new challenge. The analogy Joe uses for our effort at the time is that of a hamster on a wheel: all we were thinking about was our next step and the one after that. We didn't have the luxury of thinking about how to get from here to there—we were still operating with the mindset of "What do I need to do to stay alive today?" Joe described the business as "death by a thousand cuts." He was right, of course.

Maybe the only difference was that by then, I was so torn up that I no longer felt the pain as I once had.

The expectation was that, with the help of RoundTable, we would reach the next level. The reality was that we were still fighting a war that involved a significant amount of hand-to-hand combat. We had been receiving cease-and-desist warnings from Medtronic for months. With RoundTable behind us, I finally felt comfortable balling up those letters and tossing them in the trash. Our Stryker contact—somewhat affectionately nicknamed Deep Throat—who'd been quietly calling Mark Solomon for months and sharing information about his company's interest in Vanguard, went quiet after RoundTable came into play. Everyone knew that with RoundTable on our side, we would benefit from Joe's experience and reputation.

What also came with the deal were contacts. I remember going to a ballgame at Wrigley Field with Joe and Tommy Thompson, secretary of Health and Human Services. Perhaps most importantly, from the perspective of the Big Dogs, Vanguard now had the financial runway to outlast any of their tactics. The war could linger for as long as they were willing to keep fighting, but Vanguard would endure.

CHAPTER 15

THE LONG ROAD TO LEGITIMACY

You may have to fight a battle more than once to win it.
— Margaret Thatcher

After Marge and I hosted the cocktail party at the NASPE conference in New Orleans—the one where Scott Wait made his announcement about Illinois—I realized he might be correct and that the business was indeed "fragile."

If I'm being honest with myself, I was more than a little concerned that night. I had once told Marge that if she promised not to worry, I would do the worrying for both of us. Her response? "No, Chuck. I can't depend on you to do the worrying. *I* will do it!"

The bill that had been introduced by Senator Bowles was just one step away from passing and could not be ignored, even by me. This was a clear and very troubling escalation in the war with the Big Dogs, and could easily have made them the victors—had they known about what was happening in Illinois.

The bill had flown through the Illinois Senate, but thankfully we got wind of it right around the time it reached a house committee. We were thankful and somewhat surprised that the Big Dogs were unaware of the existence of the bill, which they could have used as legal leverage, causing a ripple effect of state rulings against SUD reprocessing.

Acutely aware that time was of the essence in a way that it had never been before, we went into action on the Monday after returning from New Orleans. AMDR put a team together and flew up to Springfield, Illinois. We retained a lobbyist, Carol Dart, who for five thousand dollars agreed to represent us in the battle to have reprocessing outlawed. It was a check Vanguard couldn't afford to write, but in the heat of the battle, we couldn't afford *not* to write it either. Failing to direct every resource toward our survival meant inescapable death.

The strategy was to get the Illinois Hospital Association engaged in defeating the bill by suggesting that its passing would only end up hurting their hospitals. Getting the eight-hundred-pound gorilla on our side took no longer than ten minutes, and having it on our side didn't go unnoticed by Senator Bowles, who later noted that when her bill hit the radar screen, hospital people came flying in from all over to try to dissuade her.

There's no doubt that providence once again played a hand. Had our Chicago rep not called Scott to see if he knew about the senator's bill, and had we not looked bigger than we actually were to the Illinois Hospital Association, we wouldn't have been able to get them in our corner. Were it not for these fortuitous events, we likely wouldn't have been able to secure the safe harbor provision that ultimately saved our bacon.

Lobbyist to lobbyist, we met with Senator Bowles and convinced her to change just one sentence in her bill, the one that read "No entity can reprocess medical devices labeled single use," to "No entity can reprocess a medical device labeled single use *unless it is a hospital or a medical device company that is registered with the FDA.*" This single concession effectively neutralized the bill, so far as the operations of AMDR's members were concerned. These were, of course, the only entities doing reprocessing anyway. Nothing changed for us, Senator Bowles was satisfied, and Vanguard was free to get back to business.

Of course, just because you set your sail doesn't mean the wind won't change. We next found ourselves fighting a similar battle in California. Our victory there came thanks to a more nuanced conflict of personalities. Though the Big Dogs tried to use science to bolster their argument, they soon discovered that facts refuse to yield to even the most vehement argument if it rests only on emotion.

Mark, who had been media-trained by Ethicon, perhaps knew better than anyone that it was about the questions more than the answers. Mark understood that the other side had to be permitted to express their needs and problems, even when doing so exasperated both them and us. He was also very much aware that extraordinarily personal agendas were at work. His words could be twisted to such a degree that he alone could bring down the entire fledgling industry by saying the wrong thing. For instance, if a reporter asked him, "Do you realize reprocessed devices could kill babies?" Mark knew there was no way he could repeat the phrase "kill babies." He had to reply with a truthful but neutral statement, such as "Our safety record is perfect."

We were experts in sterilization, and there was no need to be afraid. However, Mark appreciated the reach and influence of the Big Dogs' PR and marketing budgets. In much the same way as the Big Dogs would plant high-powered surgical nurse consultants to ask leading questions designed to trip us up during meetings, so reporters could be fed questions intended to lead us into a very public trap.

Many of the leaders in our industry had seen Mark present the science of reprocessing of medical devices labeled single use at medical centers, physician meetings, and trade shows. We intimately understood the science and had full confidence in it. However, Mark was under tremendous pressure as the public face of reprocessing and found himself to never be truly off the record. Mark recalls having to sometimes even field questions when he used the men's restroom!

When California came into play, Mark and I had to once again get on a plane to go defend our company, and in fact, the whole industry. It was critical that we all were on the same page, and that legislators got it from the top—not just from the leadership of Vanguard, but from the entire SUD reprocessing industry. The fear that all we had worked for could be destroyed was very real. A single loss in a single state had the potential to awaken an avalanche of political objections that could cripple us nationwide. It was, to some degree, like Illinois over and over again, our very own Groundhog Day.

We were once again represented by AMDR and secured lobbyists. On the Big Dogs' side were more lobbyists and representation by the Health Industry Manufacturers Association. Both sides quickly discovered that there are two distinct Californias as far as beliefs and attitudes were concerned. A Jewish doctor brought in from New York asserted that allowing reprocessing in California was akin to committing medical malpractice. His perspective might have garnered support from a doctor hailing from Southern California, while a doctor in attendance from Northern California, who could best be described as a good old boy, didn't take kindly to an East Coast doctor telling him how medicine should be practiced in California.

As a result, the legal fight was over in California before it really got started. We knew it and they knew it. The evening following the Northern California doctor's dressing-down of his East Coast peer, the Big Dogs' lobbyist called our lobbyist and admitted, "Your guy kicked our ass." Once again, we had a force behind us that ensured no one would be swayed by even the most forceful fearmongering rhetoric.

The next attempt, focused on Florida, is one I don't recall much about because it was so feeble. There was a meeting or two, but these never went anywhere, much to the Big Dogs' displeasure. The next offensive was another matter. The Big Dogs thought they could finally get us in their jaws at the federal level.

It took a full year, during which the Big Dogs clung to their belief that regulation would do us in. Then the Medical Device User Fee and Modernization Act (MDUFMA) went before a congressional committee. According to the FDA, in the run-up to 2002, the FDA's medical device program was suffering from a long-term, significant loss of resources that was undermining the program's capacity and performance. In early 2002, the medical device industry and Congress recognized that the program needed additional resources. Approval of 510(k) applications was taking too long, and expertise was still not readily available.

In response, leaders of the SUD reprocessing industry approached the FDA and Congress to initiate discussions about linking new user fees to increased appropriations in order to augment the resources available for device review. Congress concluded that the FDA resources were limited, and without a new infusion of funding review times would likely increase in the future.

Congress, the FDA, and the industry therefore worked together to develop a solution. The framework for MDUFMA was agreed on before October 26, 2002, the date on which the congressional act was signed into law. In small part, the act reads:

The Congress finds that—

(1) Prompt approval and clearance of safe and effective devices is critical to the improvement of the public health so that patients may enjoy the benefits of devices to diagnose, treat, and prevent disease;

(2) The public health will be served by making additional funds available for the purpose of augmenting the resources of the Food and Drug Administration that are devoted to the process for the review of devices and the assurance of device safety and effectiveness so that statutorily mandated deadlines may be met; and

(3) The fees authorized by this title will be dedicated to meeting the goals identified in the letters from the Secretary of Health and Human Services and the Committee on Energy and Commerce of the House of Representatives and the Committee on Health, Education, Labor, and Pensions of the Senate, as set forth in the Congressional Record.

This act made certain that the FDA would have the necessary resources to ensure that safe and effective devices were being introduced to the market in a timely manner. With the acknowledgment that reprocessed SUDs would *officially* be considered as safe and effective as original devices, what we had always known and had always been able to prove became a legitimate practice.

There was no celebration. We simply let out a shared sigh of relief. Back when we had managed to amend the bill introduced by

Senator Bowles in Illinois, we'd been jubilant. When that bill was rendered harmless, Bill Stover and I had embraced, as had Mark and Kerry Hicks. But Mike Mayry was a different story. When Hicks, as the Paragon sales manager, walked over to shake his hand, the expression on Mike's face made clear how he felt. Mike in his words was fine with the rest of us having our "lovey-dovey stuff," but he and the Paragon sales manager had a fight on their hands.

With the passage of MDUFMA, we found ourselves back in the familiar territory of trying to distinguish ourselves from our competition. To the victor go the spoils.

As for the Big Dogs? Well, the bigger they are, the harder they fall. With their tails between their legs, our enemies were forced to retreat.

Vanguard 1, Big Dogs 0.

Joe and I had the same reaction: "*Now* we've got a business!"

The Big Dogs weren't about to welcome us into their pack, and they were certainly not about to return to the porch to lick their wounds. There would be no time for anyone to heal up before they launched one final, desperate attack.

Part IV

Victory Is Ours

Here's my strategy...we win, they lose.

— Ronald Reagan

CHAPTER 16

A NEW MISSION

Leadership is about vision and responsibility, not power.
— Seth Berkley

"She's feeling nervous about coming in here to speak with you, Chuck," John Sabat said from across my desk. Since signing on as human resources director, he had been able to balance the needs of the employees and the needs of the company in a way that his predecessor, Henry Philpott, had never quite achieved. Henry's concern for Vanguard's employees had been commendable and his care invaluable when we were still a small company suffering from small problems. John is the son of a union leader; he had early career experience in directly taking on a union. John knew the law *and* he knew how to protect the company and its employees in the kinds of increasingly knotty situations that arise in a rapidly growing operation.

So, when John mentioned that one of the production workers had an issue that I needed to address right away, I looked up from what I'd been half-focusing on (the other half of my focus had already been directed on John).

I have always prided myself on being a good listener. I learned early in life that when I spent time with girls, unlike boys, the fists didn't usually fly. Juli Schroble, my junior prom date, had made me feel included and welcome. I returned the kindness simply by listening. My mother had told me, "It doesn't cost anything to listen, and you'll learn about the things people deeply care about and need to express. People need and deserve to be able to share the things that are on their minds and in their hearts."

"Yeah, no problem," I said to John, pushing aside the financials I'd been scrutinizing. For now, the battles with the Big Dogs had ended, but the financial aftermath had to be dealt with. We were certain to burn through a significant amount of RoundTable's $12 million investment. The opportunity to put one of our line workers at ease was a welcome distraction; unlike the company's cash flow, this problem was within my power to solve.

Our first production worker, Vicky Kennedy, had gone on to join Mark's key product management team, tasked alongside Lee Rose with finding and developing new products. Our current group of line workers had swelled to triple digits. Across the board, the plant's production workers had almost always been women. Whether an employee was male or female, however, my leadership style remained the same. That was a good thing, because we were on the brink of hiring our first female executive for the position of CFO, one of the most important roles in the company.

No matter the role or the responsibilities involved, I also never failed to take an interest in our employees' personal lives. If family issues required time away from work, the culture of the company was such that days off or even extended periods of time to tend to these concerns was wholeheartedly supported. Anytime I hired an executive, I wanted to meet his or her spouse or significant other. I knew that if there wasn't support in the relationship, it was just a matter of time before that executive's home life spilled over into the job and would have an effect on their performance, which could negatively impact the greater company.

To keep my fingers on the emotional pulse of my employees, I practiced an open-door policy and made myself available to counsel the people for whom I felt responsible. I have always believed that, though I had the honor of marching in front of the band, the employees were the ones making the music.

In the early days of Vanguard, it was much easier to stay in immediate contact with everyone, as I could count on my hands the total number of its employees. Right from the start, we double-dated with husbands and wives, watched one another's dogs during vacations, and laughed at the same inside jokes. We cried when someone had to be let go. We paid, anonymously, for needed car repairs. We even wrote personal checks for one another during those times when paychecks wouldn't stretch far enough. We were the family we made—a family I was proud to lead.

So, I continued to be surprised when employees found it difficult to come into my office to talk with me about their concerns. Of course, I was also taken aback when employees expressed concern or were offended when we passed each other in the building and I didn't acknowledge them. I never intentionally ignored anyone, but my mind moved just as quickly as my legs, and I often simply failed to register their presence.

Multiple tiers had been added to the company hierarchy as it continued to grow. More and more of my employees were unfamiliar to me. Vanguard had fought tooth and nail to generate demand, but to meet that rising demand, we'd hired so many people that I was no longer intimately familiar with every one of them— nor they with me. Increasingly, I understood that employees, especially new ones, perceived a distance between them and me.

They hadn't come in to work to find Doug sleeping on his office floor. They hadn't noticed Mark's absence during the year he was deployed in DC. They had no sense of my struggle to make payroll every two weeks.

And now that Vanguard was operated by RoundTable, employees' reluctance to engage with the leadership was sure to increase. People instinctively fear what they don't know. If Vanguard's internal growth had proved a hurdle for them, the involvement of RoundTable was sure to be a barrier that some would not be able to overcome.

* * *

"You need to make her feel comfortable," John said. "Be calming and soft-spoken. Hear her out."

Calming and soft-spoken, I mused.

"It's difficult for her to come in here and speak with the boss, the person who signs her checks," John continued earnestly.

I can be calming and soft-spoken, I thought as I turned my back on the numbers I'd been reviewing. *No problem.*

As he walked out of my office, John called over his shoulder, "Remember, Chuck, don't be intimidating."

And I wasn't intimidating. I made sure of that. My conversation with the production worker ended with me feeling pretty good about how it went, and quite proud of my calming and soft-spoken demeanor. Judging from the line worker's reaction, I had excelled. I'd nodded a lot and offered plenty of genuine, gentle smiles. I'd been still and composed. I had even tried to make myself as physically small as possible. There was little doubt that I had come across as impressively nonthreatening, my entire aura almost

Zen-like. It had felt good to make a connection and offer some assistance.

It didn't take long for John to check in and ask how, from my perspective, things had gone. As he took a seat in my office, I repeated for him the entire—productive, I thought—discussion. Then, with my chest puffed out, I confidently asked him, "So, how do you think I did? How was I?"

"Eh," John said. My bubble deflated even before he got to "You were okay."

* * *

On the battlefield, a leader must be decisive. But the true nature of the role is to be a supreme encourager. I had spent so long fighting alongside my employees that I'd honed my troop-encouraging skills, and of course it's never a challenge to sanction and support something you believe in with your entire being. It isn't difficult to want the best for others when you truly respect them and value their contributions to the team effort.

Yet when that same leader finds himself in the war room, he must be able to make difficult decisions. This is why I admire Winston Churchill: he could make the hard decisions. A war is a war, no matter where it's fought, and in any war, the paramount need is for decisiveness. Being clear-minded about making decisions is ultimately how you mobilize an army.

With the arrival of our own Big Dog, in the form of RoundTable, our mission had changed irrevocably. We were no longer fighting to survive the Big Dogs; we were seeking to run with them. The passing of MDUFMA had leveled the battlefield. Our new directive was to keep up. We certainly weren't looking to be welcomed into the pack, and we didn't want to join them in the shade of the porch. Our victory would come when one of them bought us.

All the tactics the Big Dogs had unleashed on us had not only proven that we could survive their best shots, but that their former stranglehold on hospitals had been released. If they wanted to regain some of that strength, they needed to consolidate it by buying us out of the business. As we saw it, we who had championed SUD reprocessing should and would prosper as a result. The Big Dogs would finally get some slumber back on the porch, but not before ensuring that we retreated from the fence line where our conflict with them had first raged.

For this to come to pass, every decision our company made from this point forward would have to be in support of this aim. Whether those decisions involved laying off employees who had fought alongside me in the trenches, or included *all* of us having to follow the commands of a different leader, there were more tough calls to be made at this time than at any other in Vanguard's history. Thankfully, a leader can both care deeply about his troops and be unafraid of doing what's right for the overall mission.

I had proudly fought shoulder to shoulder with the Vanguard soldiers. Together we had launched an industry, resulting in the creation of many American jobs. We had reprocessed millions of devices and generated value for thousands of customers, all the while upholding the highest standards of quality and patient safety. Half a billion pounds of biohazardous waste had escaped our landfills, thanks to our green process.

There was no doubt that accepting RoundTable's investment was the right thing for the company, and I don't ever recall expecting that there would be pushback from employees. It certainly wasn't my expectation that we'd all be popping champagne, but I likewise never expected that I'd have to sell anyone on what RoundTable was bringing to the proverbial table. I wholly believed in what I was evangelizing—RoundTable was *the* ally that would get us off the battlefield and into a lasting peacetime.

Therefore, it wasn't surprising to me that Joe Damico described the reception he received from Vanguard employees as one of open arms. Given the character of the people I'd come to know, I wouldn't have expected anything less from them. They were wonderful, caring, deeply committed individuals whom I respected and trusted.

Yet I also couldn't delude myself. Apart from those who'd been trained in warfighting by the Big Dogs themselves, like Mark, Mike Mayry and Mary Vermillion, these were also people who had never done anything on the RoundTable level. We were, by now, brothers and sisters in arms. In any war, there are bound to be losses, and if another commander has a more expansive view of the battlefield, a change in leadership is almost certain to occur.

I was blessed that our employees considered me the skeleton on which they could depend, because the Vanguard body was about to morph. Although I have been described as "unflappable" and am said to project my confidence to everyone else, I know that change is unsettling at best and at worst a very destructive force within a company. Not everyone is able to keep their vision trained ahead as they maintain momentum in the same direction. I'd perfected this skill, growing up in my dad's household. I could choose to mentally tally all of the fights I'd been forced to survive, or I could count down only those fights that remained until I was out of the house and free.

The success we had fought so hard for could be at risk if people decided they didn't want other leaders to join our very tight ranks. I didn't blame them. After all, seeing the bigger picture is difficult when your view of the battlefield is limited to the few feet in front of you. Nevertheless, these were people who wanted to be successful. The Vanguard employees might have been intimidated by the experience, knowledge, and wealth that RoundTable was contributing to the war effort, but they could also discern that these things were likely to be our salvation. Although they understood it in varying degrees, our employees did recognize that they didn't have what it took to get Vanguard where we wanted it to go.

When he stepped in, Joe wasn't surprised to find limited systems and processes in place, or that only a minor amount of training, coaching, and development had been undertaken. There were no one- or five-year plans in place. We were a cash in, cash out business in Lakeland, Florida, just audacious enough to discover something worth fighting for and, like scrappy terriers, refusing to relent. Joe understood that when you're caught in a gun battle, there isn't much opportunity to pull back and pore over a battlefield map in order to plan your next angle of attack. We had been fighting so long and so hard for survival that every day was an accomplishment. Strategizing for the long game was impossible and, quite frankly, unimaginable.

While there was no doubt that we needed RoundTable's injection of cash and energy, Vanguard's employees thankfully still possessed their original commitment, passion, and integrity. Because they were accustomed to operating with no margin of error, they achieved the highest of standards.

We were about to discover that supporting a new mission can look and feel very different.

It had taken Vanguard a decade to get to $10 million in annual revenue. It wasn't that what we had been doing hadn't been working; it just wasn't working fast enough. If you're only selling one product at a time, the cost of business becomes too high and the company's growth is too slow. You can gain customers and close deals—you can be successfully selling, as I had done all those years ago in North Carolina as an independent rep for Sterile Design—but a company can easily collapse under the weight of its own operating costs. Vanguard's systems had been built to stand up under the scrutiny of the highest level of government oversight, but we weren't able to keep ahead of the costs required to keep us toe to toe with the FDA.

We needed to get bigger, to approximately $100 million in annual revenue. Joe briefed us that this was the plan—not to continue to grow incrementally, but instead to do something more dramatic. Any potential buyout of the company needed to be worth the cost of the lawyers that would be involved. For this to happen, we had to bring in ten times the revenue, and achieve that goal in less than half of the time it had taken us to reach $10 million. Joe appreciated that MDUFMA had created more demand for what we were doing, and that there was good reason to do things differently than we'd been doing them all along. We were now in a race against time.

As quickly as possible, we needed to isolate the tipping point of our customers' confidence in our commitment to ensuring good and safe clinical outcomes for their patients and cost savings for their facilities. Our moment-of-truth question had become "How can we get customers to stop assessing the risks and give us enough of their business so that SUD reprocessing gets integrated into their financial and clinical frameworks?"

Joe knew that, while Vanguard primarily needed an infusion of cash, we also needed to bring in people who had experience with scaling a business and could keep a watchful eye on the investment dollars while this was happening. The people Joe had in mind had just come from running much bigger companies and had sales and management training in Fortune 500 companies. As Joe asserts, you spend the same amount of time and energy on a company making $10 million as you do on one making $100 million. So, leaders of this caliber were necessary right from the start.

Vanguard's employees had long been driven by the conviction that they were doing the right thing for the right reasons. They deserved to make as much money from the company's sale as possible. If Joe said that we needed to find people with a growth perspective and hands-on experience with scaling, then that was precisely what we were going to do to ensure that *every employee* would prosper when the company was eventually sold—whether or not they were still employed at the time of that sale.

Joe vividly recalls one of the conversations he had with me about bringing on new blood—specifically, hiring three of his most trusted leaders—and being pleasantly surprised at the ease of my response. I said, "Okay, Joe, if you think we need to upgrade our talent to get to the next level, and you have those types of people, then let's do it."

CHAPTER 17

MUSCLING UP

A single person doesn't change an organization, but culture and good people do.

— Frances Hesselbein

Our first step toward achieving the kind of growth our new mission demanded was to figure out why Vanguard was the size it was. Maybe there hadn't been enough investment in the sales force. Maybe manufacturing and labor had become bloated. Or maybe vision had been lacking. As any investor knows, it's only when you isolate the cause of the limitations you face that you can start to think about implementing solutions for growth.

RoundTable had done its due diligence, and Joe knew that they had the resources Vanguard needed. Equally important, he had confidence that our science was sound. But Joe always believed that Vanguard was living on a precipice; we were one defect away from being out of business. It was our built-in tracking controls that gave him at least a measure of comfort in that regard.

Still, there was little doubt that investing in Vanguard was more of an adventure for RoundTable than an investment in an ongoing, established, cash flow-positive company. We were successfully selling our service, so we had proven that there was indeed an appetite for it. Joe readily admits that he and his fellow cofounders were a bit naive, in that they were entirely convinced that SUD reprocessing in general, and Vanguard specifically, had a home within the industry.

Joe and his partners had spent a lot of time in a tangential business, and had seen it grow from nothing to one billion dollars. So, despite some initial apprehension about Vanguard's size, Joe remained convinced that there was an opportunity in Vanguard and in the SUD reprocessing industry. Because of my microbiology background, there was science to back him up.

I would therefore continue to be the face of the company for its employees. I would also be coaching new arrivals about the science and continuing to sell it to increasingly influential customers. On more than a few occasions during important plant tours, Joe would whisper at me to put on my lab coat and "try to look scientific." There was work to be done if I was going to take that coat off once and for all.

Most business founders who continue to serve as CEOs have an office or plant within thirty minutes' drive from their home. They are therefore mostly confined to finding talent within that half-hour radius. RoundTable, on the other hand, could draw talent from across the nation. Their desire to shore up the business by bringing in new talent wasn't to suggest that their people were somehow superior. We simply needed individuals with experience. There's a skill set to growing a company quickly while keeping operating costs low. In order for the Big Dogs to pick up on our for-sale scent, we needed to hit the magic annual revenue number of $100 million.

There was little choice but for Joe's most trusted team members—a triumvirate of sales, production, and finance functions—to come on board. Joe was correct, however, when he said that if anyone at Vanguard were to spend even a minimal amount of time with these fine leaders and equally fine people, they would come away from the experience a fan. Joe knew that if none of the Vanguard employees felt comfortable bringing his people home for dinner, they weren't the right fit for the company. Although he didn't have to do it, the fact that Joe gave me the chance to interview and offer my thoughts on the hiring of these individuals said a lot about who he is as a man and leader.

The first to come in for an interview was Mac Brown, who had started out as a systems manager, installing and maintaining computers in hospitals. The things he was working on—sales information and sales volume—brought him into contact with sales reps who were, at that time, making hundreds of thousands of dollars a year. *Whatever that job is*, Mac thought, *I gotta do that*. So, he shifted his career to sales and sales management.

He had endured what he calls the "fantastic crucible of leadership" at American Hospital Supply, a company he believes prepared him well for his future career. Through a series of mergers and acquisitions and ever-increasing responsibilities, Mac ended up as one of the top performers and business leaders inside Allegiance, directed by the man who was also his mentor and friend, Joe Damico.

During Mac's first retirement, while he was running his own real estate business, Joe called and invited him for a round of golf. Mac had been close with Joe ever since he found himself stuck in brutally cold Chicago one holiday weekend. Joe had invited him to his house to hang out and watch some sports.

Knowing Joe like he did, Mac could tell that there was something on his mind during this apparently casual round of golf. Toward the end, he finally asked Joe what was going on.

"We just made an acquisition of a new company," Joe said.

Mac, of course, knew all about Joe and his partners forming RoundTable, aptly named because when people are seated at a round table, everyone is equal.

"Well, that's great, Joe. What does the company do?"

"They reprocess single-use devices."

At this, Mac paused and looked at Joe, before in all seriousness asking, "What would you want to do that for? That's insane!"

"I know, I know," Joe said, though there was a glimmer in his eye that suggested he believed otherwise.

That glimmer, however, was not enough to sway Mac. "I'm not interested," he said. Then, softening a little because of his appreciation for Joe's goodwill, Mac explained, "My business is going well, and that part of my medical career has kind of gone by. I'm enjoying managing the real estate business. Thank you, Joe. Once again, I'm so appreciative that you would want me to be involved, but I'm just not sure about this."

"I tell you what," Joe said. "Why don't you go out there and meet them. I just bought a company about forty minutes away from your door. You have to at least go and *look*. Tell me what you think. Even if you're not going to be a part of it, you can give me your impressions."

"Okay," Mac said. "That's fair."

So Mac came out to Lakeland, where he spent the day touring the plant, meeting me, and talking with many of us to learn our story. Mac had come up through the enemy camp, but he instantly recognized the value in what we were doing and instinctively *got* the business. I had the suspicion that Mac was intrigued. This sense was swiftly proven correct.

As he explains it, Mac took one look at our business—and at me— called up Joe, and said, "Okay, I'm going to help." The very next day, Mac drove out to the plant, negotiated his salary, and started working with us. Just like that, he was all in.

With dirt under his fingernails, Tony O'Neill was the prototypical manufacturing guy. In his previous job, Tony had managed seven plants. Although he had recently overseen production for a $7 billion company, the hands-on aspect of an operation many times smaller in size and scope was exciting to him. Tony knew Joe from their Cardinal days and trusted that if he did a good job at Vanguard, RoundTable would take care of him.

Tony was therefore brought in to lead operations. For this task, one that from Joe's perspective involved "moving mountains," Tony had the critical production, materials, and logistics experience. His task was to develop the processes that would ultimately please the customer. This objective included receiving, reprocessing, and shipping products, and doing it all quickly so that customers weren't waiting long. This was a pivotal move away from the dry-cleaner model of service to the rapid-return model, which would come into play as the ultimate differentiator between us and our competition.

Finding a better model than the one our competitors were using wasn't easy, but it was groundbreaking. In the dry-cleaning model, the customer gave us, for example, five devices. That customer then had to wait however long it took for those five devices to go through our various processing systems—in some cases weeks. When the devices were ready, we called the customer and, taking into account shipping time, provided the estimated time frame in which they could expect to receive their newly reprocessed devices. The customer had no way of knowing when to expect our call or whether all five devices had been accepted for reprocessing and would be returned to them.

The dry-cleaning model had become a major impediment for us doing the kind of high-volume reprocessing we needed to grow our annual revenue. It was also limiting to the customer. A materials manager was likely to go out and buy new devices once the wait got to be too much to handle.

We couldn't just sit back and allow our customers to buy new products from the Big Dogs. We had to find a way to deliver the devices they wanted when they wanted them. We had to ensure that they no longer received phone calls that told them, "Well, you gave us five trocars, and we're sending you back four—oh, and those four trocars will arrive in a week, as long as there aren't any shipping delays."

It was no easy birth, but the rapid-return model was eventually born. With this shift, customers got immediate credit for their devices and were able to buy right away from our existing stock. A standard rejection rate, calculated by Steve's Magic software, was applied up front, so there were no surprises down the line. The customer could send us ten devices, get immediate credit, and able to purchase eight—and those eight would be shipped immediately.

But first we had to get customers to buy in to the system's potential benefits. In addition to having to physically pull and process all of the devices together, we also had to push back against the notion that some hospitals' products were cleaner than others. For a time, we had to run a separate production line for those customers who resisted. Eventually, though, the benefit of a known and equally applied rejection ratio—not to mention a faster turnaround—turned all of our customers into converts.

Tony soon realized that the combination of our expedited processes and a new selling strategy meant that the sales cycle was going to be longer than we were used to, and that when those orders started coming in, they would be bigger than we had ever seen. Achieving the balance between waiting longer for sales and then having a large enough supply to fulfill orders immediately was going to be every bit as difficult as running seven plants for a multibillion-dollar company.

There is something to be said for the ingenuity that you're forced to exercise when it feels like you're bumping up against every possible constraint. Establishing a smooth and less-costly product flow was an immediate concern for Tony. Despite having a more mature presentation, the issue was no less problematic than the types of product-flow problems that had once plagued pre-investment Vanguard.

In 1997, UPS went on strike. The sixteen days during which they shut down operations cost UPS hundreds of millions of dollars and put a major strain on those of us who relied on their service. Although alternate carriers would carry packages, those companies were rationing the number of packages they would handle. This meant that on the Vanguard receiving dock, only about half the number of packages were coming in. This was obviously an impediment for any business, but more so for us because the source of our raw material was shipments from hospitals.

It didn't take long for these hospitals to tire of those raw materials—the SUDs to be reprocessed—sitting on their floors and waiting to be picked up. Within two days of the start of the strike, they started calling us up and saying that if we didn't pick up the devices, they were going into the trash.

Well, if there isn't any work for the employees, then there's nothing for the company to invoice. Those of us in Lakeland could drive around to area hospitals and do those pickups and deliveries ourselves, but Mary Vermillion and Scott Wait were doing a lot of business in the St. Louis area. They knew that even if they could pick up devices from their clients, there was no way to reprocess them. They also knew that we couldn't lose this business. So, they looked at each other and asked, "What are we going to do?"

Thanks to the availability of U-Hauls, there was no need for us to turn our destiny over to a labor dispute. The St. Louis reps took matters quite literally into their own hands by going from hospital to hospital to collect the devices, loading the devices onto U-Haul trucks, and hiring drivers to get the loads down to Lakeland. The reprocessed loads were driven back up to St. Louis to be personally hand-delivered.

Life under RoundTable was different, but the need to get products from and to hospitals without delay wasn't. Tony understood that what had changed since the nineties was the rising pressure surrounding costs; hospitals were getting squeezed like never before. Thanks to our newfound ability to directly target the C-suite (the hospital's upper management which includes the CEO, CFO, and COO), hospital executives quickly understood our value proposition, and jumped right in to liberate themselves from the financial grip of Big Dog pricing.

Even so, during our sales meetings, customer commitment to their patients typically meant that hospitals wanted to revisit the science in more detail. For this reason, we believed in the value of direct clinician-to-clinician communication. We had a high level of confidence in Mac's system because it had worked multiple times during his career of selling solely to hospitals and health systems.

He hired new salespeople and personally trained the existing salespeople in his way of selling. What we didn't have, despite our high level of across-the-board expertise, were all the answers. It simply wasn't possible when the stench of misinformation lingered, left over from the prolonged war with the Big Dogs.

* * *

For those answers, we brought in Deb Haley, a whip-smart perioperative director who, as a nurse, understood better than any of us the things that mattered most to clinicians. She brought instant credibility to our team. We could say, "Let me introduce you to Deb," whenever we were asked some version of the question "Well, how are you going to do that?" Deb was equally respected by hospitals for whom the primary focus was patient safety. Anytime someone of Deb's caliber is involved, you're not just saying to a customer that you're confident—you are saying that you're credible.

Thankfully, clinician presence was never perceived as a sales tool or marketing ploy. I can't recall the number of times I gave my introduction and five-minute spiel before stepping aside to give the floor to Deb. The customer knew she talked the talk of C-suite presentations and walked the walk of a surgical nurse. Whenever Deb was in the room, there was the definite sense that *she* was the person everyone wanted to hear from. I was explicitly told so, time and time again.

* * *

I was also immensely impressed by Barb Sullivan the first time I met her. But I did voice one concern to Tony after the interview was over. "Listen. Barb's great—she's sharp and bubbly, and just a genuinely good fit for the CFO role."

"But?" Tony said.

"The problem is … maybe she's too young."

"Maybe the problem is you're too old," Tony accurately deadpanned.

This was right around the time I was starting to more acutely feel the aches and pains brought on by all the years of fighting. Mac and Barb and Tony came in and made everything new again. They invited me to feed off their energy.

It would have been one thing if the new leadership team had gone out of their way to make employees feel comfortable that they still reported to me, only to go around or behind me whenever it was necessary to achieve some end that I was impeding. But this was never an issue since Mac, Tony and Barb, were each one a class act. They were respectful about talking directly with me and including me in tactical and strategic planning.

These were three people who were accustomed to showing up on set, assessing the work, and getting on with it. There were no games, nor time to play them. As the consummate sales manager, Mac took analytics to Barb. She would sometimes challenge him on financial grounds, though always in her typical pleasant way. Tony taught us production, giving us a master class in something we thought we knew. Showing respect and feeling respected were never issues among us—even when Tony and I disagreed on the value of a tunnel dryer for drying sequential compression devices. A tunnel dryer didn't have the same propensity to damage them like the clothes dryers we'd always used. I don't recall how that friendly argument was settled, though I imagine Joe had an ever-steady hand in its resolution.

I do remember when Joe made the suggestion that I interview Mac for sales and marketing, a position that would make him Mark's boss. Mark was out of the office when I sat down with Mac, but there was a window of time during which the two of them would be at the airport and could make a conversation happen. I therefore recommended that Mark meet with Mac, and he gladly obliged.

Early the next morning I followed up with Mark. "Well, what did you think of Mac?"

"Oh man, Chuck, yeah, yeah," Mark replied. He no doubt recognized Mac's elite sales training, as Mark was never shy about being an Ethicon guy. "Yeah, no, he's great," Mark continued, before catching himself and asking, "But what role is he interviewing for?"

CHAPTER 18

TRIBAL KNOWLEDGE

A candle loses nothing by lighting another candle.
— Father James Keller

Although the Vanguard management and sales teams needed shoring up—a fact I never disputed, since I had hired my friends and former business associates before I even knew if we *had* a business—Joe never considered bringing in new blood without keeping me on as the steady skeleton of this rejuvenated body. I continued as CEO, and Joe served as chairman.

For many entrepreneurs, reporting to someone else is something their ego won't allow. I can honestly say, though, that I had no problem with having a boss at that point—especially a boss like Joe. Although this shake-up (the first of many) might have been viewed by some of the employees as me becoming sandwiched between RoundTable subordinates and superiors, I found some relief in other people's involvement in decision-making and implementation.

Joe has been in the industry for forty years, and as such understands better than most how people naturally want to complicate things. The RoundTable aim with Vanguard (and with every company they invest in) is to keep things simple: get the best people and give them the resources they need, treat the customer right, and take care of the employees.

The other passion for Joe was not making dumb decisions. Or at least try to limit them. Leaders are accustomed to making a thousand little decisions every day. The beauty of small decisions is that any damage they cause is going to be minimal. When you make big decisions and get even one wrong, you can make life very hard for yourself and for your people. Joe believed that if only 80 percent of our decisions were the right ones, we would still be just fine. The RoundTable people were used to having significant resources at their disposal; they typically wouldn't bat an eye at making a $2 million decision that could turn out wrong.

This was where their new approach was so helpful. Every Vanguard employee had been well aware of how even a single minor decision could push us over the precipice from *emergent* company to *expired* company. So, all the knowledge that had been organically built into our business family needed to be conferred upon the new members without delay. It likely wouldn't have unfolded that way in most other companies, but few Vanguard employees believed that by sharing the ingredients of our secret sauce, we were betraying the family heritage or working ourselves out of a job. We wanted to share, and we were fortunate to have new additions to the family who wanted to learn because, as they saw it, they wanted to be successful with us.

The notion that the RoundTable superstars must have been given a boatload in stock options to lure them down to this little company in Lakeland was quickly dispelled by their eagerness to learn from us and their willingness to work long hours alongside us. There was a lot of new energy, with new ideas and new directions. However, in working to make us world class, these seasoned professionals never made a show of their power. We were an expanded team, and were now the right team, all of us teaching, coaching, and learning from each other. Because we all genuinely enjoyed one another, it didn't take long before it was us against the world.

* * *

Mac's major desire had always been to become a doctor. He was a research scientist all the way through college, and his microbiological research had helped him pay for his degree. Therefore, he had the background to very quickly realize that I wasn't just a guy with a wild idea—well, it was a little wild—but I could also speak to the science in great detail. More importantly, what I was saying had been proven correct by the FDA itself. After a very successful career selling disposable products, Mac knew his first move was to ask me to coach him up on how to reprocess SUDs.

When Mac felt like he had a grip on the science—science he viewed as simple yet game-changing—he needed to start managing the levers he had already identified. The first lever was getting customers to the point where they believed we had a viable platform safe enough for their patients. The second lever was economic knowledge. There was no doubt that Vanguard had a financial proposition that directly and immediately benefitted hospitals. The third lever was the environment. If the cost and patient safety pieces of the equation were good, then our environmental lever was great. When we talked to customers, we'd often hear some variation of "I'm really supportive of the environment." But the next words out of their mouths would be "We can't afford to pay more for it."

We knew that hospitals were operating on less than 2 percent margins, so there was always an easy response to their fear: "You don't need to pay more—in fact, you will pay *less*!" This got their attention. They needed to put money into changing their entire model because of these new social and ecological imperatives if they wanted to keep pace with the rest of the medical industry. On top of the 30 to 50 percent we could save them on each device, it required minimal disruption to shift to reprocessed SUDs. We were really offering them twice the value for the same price.

There were two things that Mac underestimated in this business. The first was the tremendous pressure that would come from our concerned customers, who were still somewhat afraid of the unknown and of what they perceived as a potential risk to them and to their patients. He underestimated the significance of our customers' desire for risk mitigation.

Mac also had no idea how committed the Big Dogs remained, even after their hatred of Vanguard had driven them to some very irrational decisions, decisions that harmed them and caused only minimal damage to us. Looking back, Mac realizes he should have expected the hatred—after all, we had chosen to alienate the biggest and most powerful companies in the medical industry.

RoundTable was working on an assumption when they invested in us. If they didn't think they could help us, even if it was a good deal, they wouldn't do it. The assumption, therefore, was that they had the necessary resources and connections to help Vanguard, and nobody else had our knowledge. As Joe modestly explains it, RoundTable knew to invest in the few areas they knew a little about, because in those areas, they knew an awful lot of people.

Once Mac was up to speed on the nature of the customers' pushback—and more confident than ever that my conviction was rooted in verifiable science—he knew his long-cultivated relationships could come into play and benefit our sales strategy. The next task was to craft a story that was meaningful enough to catch the imaginations of the hospital's corporate leadership. These meetings with the CEO, CFO, and COO took place in what we commonly referred to as the C-Suites.

Meetings were typically scheduled for thirty minutes. In reality, that gave us only twenty minutes to get an executive to take a big conceptual leap from *That doesn't sound safe* to *Hey, that sounds like a really good idea*. First, we spoke to the science and the risks. We sought to dazzle customers with the science. We confidently told them to bring in their chief scientific officer or anyone else who was worried about the science, and we would gladly have an open dialogue with them. If they wanted to visit the plant, they were welcome to come. We knew that not a single customer would leave feeling uncomfortable about what we were doing.

It quickly became clear that Vanguard's previous selling strategy, though effective at getting us meetings, didn't have the necessary weight to ramp up our sales and processes. No longer would our message target an individual. We had to go from selling one manager one product at a time, to selling multiple product lines to a C-suite that made decisions for multiple physical facilities. We accordingly had to craft our messages to resonate with entire health systems.

The strategy was to convince these operating leaders that they wanted to tap into an industry trend that already existed: the ecological megatrend. Much of the resistance we had once encountered was already diffused, because hospitals were predisposed to support ecological responsibility. We just needed to get them to support reprocessing a specific device: a device that was labeled for single use. We could then focus on showing the raw economics of the value proposition.

Mac would take out an external fixation device (XFIX), made out of stainless steel and carbon fiber rods, and physically hold one of its connectors in his hand. These metal ball connectors sold for approximately six hundred dollars each, and several were required for each XFIX procedure. In the meeting with the customer, he would pass the connector over to the CEO or CFO, who was aware of the science and the economies that were available through reprocessing. Relying on our refined message, Mac would then say, "Okay, what you're holding is six hundred dollars' worth of carbon fiber and stainless steel—and you're throwing it away. It's external to the body, and you're just throwing it away after one use."

An executive's response to this statement was almost always a physical recoil. Mac would really drive his point home by explaining, "It is exactly the same as your brand-new Titleist driver. Would you hit one shot and then throw that driver away?"

The executives would say, "Okay, hang on. Let's go back and look at the science again."

If you were a customer worried about money, you would think primarily about savings. For those customers, the 30 to 50 percent off the cost of new products usually did the trick. For customers operating with a mindset of "patient first," their concern was the safety of the science, which was where Deb Haley came in.

But nurses were typically our first touch point at hospitals. They weren't necessarily using the products or making the decisions. The way to reach them was to talk about the environmental component of SUD reprocessing. For hospitals today it's all about cost, but twenty years ago, when the movement toward ecological responsibility was just burgeoning, being able to talk about more than money was the key to some of our success.

From Mac's perspective, however, that success didn't come fast enough. His greatest regret during his tenure at Vanguard is that he didn't act quickly enough to relieve some of the pressure caused by customers and the Big Dogs. Had he recognized that the forces being applied were going to continue past the first year, he might have adjusted the strategy. As it was, Mac's focus—just like everyone else's—was on his routine: what he had done yesterday, what he was going to do today, and how he was going to figure out just one more thing to do tomorrow.

The truth was that waiting for the tipping point at which sales volume would flow with ease took longer than RoundTable had expected, and you can only operate in that kind of intense environment for so long. It felt like, during the first half of our journey with RoundTable, we were burning through investment money just to stay afloat. Our products, though highly profitable, were not yet at the sales volume where they could support the investments that RoundTable had made in management, sales resources, and the facility itself.

To Joe, the culture of a business was paramount. With the right people in place, the right things would happen because they would be done the right way. We were driving success into every part of the system, and Joe believed that we were either arrogant enough, cocky enough, or dumb enough to trust it was eventually going to work.

Joe may have viewed me as a dynamo, albeit a *quirky* dynamo, but he also recognized that I could successfully evangelize any battle decision and rally the troops. In his opinion, humility is the single most important characteristic of a leader. Close behind that is the way you treat others, prioritizing both the customers and the people who do the actual work for you. I was happy to encourage the troops, who needed it to survive the Big Dogs' final sneak attack.

The war was over, and we had come out the victor, but we soon discovered that there were skirmishes left to fight. Thanks to RoundTable's majority stake in Vanguard, we believed we had the necessary reinforcements to head off external threats to the company. What we also had, however, was a new operating dynamic that provoked anxiety in some employees who had felt more secure with the pre-acquisition management team.

None of us had made it out of the war unscathed, but after the Big Dogs' unrelenting campaign, the Three Amigos were left especially bruised and battered. Mark Salomon, for example, had spent a solid year in DC leading the charge for regulation and navigating the land mines that kept detonating across the warfront.

There was little doubt that Mark, along with AMDR and the other invested parties responsible for MDUFMA's passage, had secured a strategic victory. But without Doug Stante's in-the-trenches battle, we would never have been able to prove to the FDA that the science supporting reprocessed SUDs was not only guaranteed safe and effective, but also made SUDs *as* safe and *as* effective as the original manufacturers' devices.

As for me, I'm always up for a good fight. Thanks in large part to the courage of my father and the unorthodox tactics of my mother, I had plenty of tenacity and mental toughness. Even after everything we had endured at Vanguard, I would *still* have dared to take on the Big Dogs, because it was a righteous fight. Yet you can only get stomped on so many times before physical and emotional fatigue sets in.

Mark, Doug, and I started to think that our elusive recovery could likely only come when the company was sold. Even more likely, we all knew, was that it was just a matter of time before the Three Amigos would be disbanded.

* * *

Doug admits that, looking back, he wouldn't have wanted Kevin Vogel's or Larry Spears's jobs; mid- and senior-level managers in the FDA who were constantly getting criticized. He also didn't want to be in front of the media cameras or congressional committees like Mark had been. Nor did he want to go out evangelizing the financial and environmental benefits of reprocessing as I did. As Doug saw it, his legacy wasn't bound to the FDA officials, who hadn't initially believed that the industry was ready for reprocessed SUDs, nor to the Big Dogs, who had wanted to squash us in order to put an end to our incursions on their revenue streams. Doug's contribution was nevertheless far greater than the data and processes he laid bare for FDA officials—surveillance that would have forced almost anyone else to shrink under the pressure.

Doug ended up leaving Vanguard abruptly for Salt Lake City, a place where he could carve out a new life for himself after years of stifling investigation and analysis. He loved living out there, nestled in the valley between the Wasatch and Oquirrh mountains. It was while living in Utah years later, and while battling cancer, that Doug watched an episode of a television show called *The Toys That Made Us*. The focus was on the designer of the *Star Wars* action figures. This man, named Ken, was responsible for a cultural phenomenon that endured for generations. In Doug's words, "How cool is the man who gets to say that?" Little has ever become known about Ken, but his influence lives on in the form of these beloved action figures.

Just like Ken, who was fired up over designing a toy that represented ingenuity, know-how, and professional achievement, Doug was the man who earned the right to say that *his* expertise and effort were responsible for SUDs being used during countless medical procedures, no doubt saving numerous lives.

Doug died on July 1, 2019, in his adopted home of Salt Lake City. In his eulogy, Seth spoke of Doug as one of the most powerful influencers on his life. His words were as emotional as they were eloquent. Listening to my oldest son describe him as the "encyclopedia on two legs" reminded me of Doug's talents and also my son's gifts. He shared one particular memory that was a perfect embodiment of Doug's singular contributions to Vanguard.

"Once, during a long day of sterilization validation, Doug and I set out for lunch in sunny Clermont, Florida. We were working in Groveland, so Clermont was sort of the big city in comparison. We were discussing the nuances of Gestalt psychology and going back and forth on our thoughts regarding this rich subject. Doug parked his truck and took a big gulp from his two-liter bottle of Diet Pepsi. (Doug really liked Diet Pepsi.) I decided to sum up our conversation.

After our long, cerebral sparring match, I stated my understanding of Gestalt psychology to Doug with these words, "You are the part and I am the whole."

As the words left my lips, Doug froze. His face turned a bright red, and that mouthful of Diet Pepsi instantly became a powder keg ready to burst. And burst it did. Diet Pepsi went everywhere, from Doug's mouth and nose it sprayed all over the car. Doug's sense of humor, clearly more sensitive than my own, resulted in that volcanic eruption of laughter and Diet Pepsi.

The central theme of our conversation leading up to that discharge of Diet Pepsi was that the whole of something is greater than the sum of its parts. This concept—applicable to many facets of our lives, including art, literature and history—gave Doug and me many days' worth of mutual pontification. As I meditated on all our shared memories and experiences, this idea kept bubbling up to the surface: *the whole is greater than the sum of its parts.*"

After spending some of Doug's last days with him, Seth recalls "a final lesson" that he received from Doug, which would come to sustain him through his grief for his mentor and father figure: *knowledge without faith is futile, and faith without knowledge is foolish.*

Many fathers have found it difficult—painful, even—to witness another man take the kind of time with their son that Doug took with Seth, but I felt blessed by it. For someone to choose to help raise your child is a gift, one I am endlessly thankful to Doug for giving to Seth and me. In Doug I lost a true friend. But when I see his influence living on through my eldest son, Doug continues to bring me great joy.

CHAPTER 19

BAND OF BROTHERS

Fire tests gold, suffering tests brave men.

— Seneca

Joe Damico and I weren't the only ones who understood that the passing of MDUFMA meant we now had a business. The Big Dogs knew it too. After we'd somehow survived against all odds to earn the FDA's "gold seal," which declared our processes just as safe and as effective as theirs, the Big Dogs knew that Vanguard no longer ran the risk of losing our existing customers. It was now going to be easy for us to add to our customer base by subtracting from theirs. We were substantially equivalent to them in every way but one: our devices were far more cost effective than theirs.

To kick up a fuss of their own, the Big Dogs introduced a number of bills at the state legislative level that proposed hospitals should be required to obtain patients' informed consent prior to any medical procedure that included the use of a reprocessed SUD. By trying to exploit any lingering concern related to the reuse of SUDs, our old enemy was doing its level best to generate false concern. Their bet was that the patient was likely to refuse to sign, and would instead demand the use of a new device.

Although every state that considered such legislation ended up rejecting it, this concerted effort by the Big Dogs' sales reps to disseminate false information about SUD reprocessing meant that fact-checking their false claims was required on an ongoing basis to keep the propaganda damage to a minimum. In this regard, AMDR proved to be our best defense. The group worked tirelessly to remind customers that reprocessed devices are equivalent to new devices, and that reprocessors are held to the same requirements as new-device manufacturers, and the FDA has declared reprocessed devices to be just as safe and effective as new devices.

The tide had turned! Thanks to MDUFMA and with the backing of AMDR, we felt secure pushing back against informed consent. We told our hospitals that if they implemented informed consent, they shouldn't bother using SUDs at all. After all, to make informed consent a requirement was effectively to state that reprocessed SUDs weren't as safe as new devices. The Big Dogs were lucky we never retaliated by raising the issue of our devices in fact being safer than theirs, since every single one of our devices—and not just a sampling, like theirs—was tested for functionality.

The Big Dogs' informed-consent campaign was ultimately nothing more than a ploy to discourage the use of reprocessed SUDs and bolster sales of their own devices. They were dropping to their knees, just as we were rising from ours. Vanguard's position on informed consent never lost us a single customer.

* * *

After having safely reprocessed over 7 million devices, Vanguard was the industry leader in the science and technology of reprocessing SUDs. The time had come at last for *us* to flex some muscle. Thanks to the uptick in our sales, influenced by MDUFMA and RoundTable, and to our status as a "portfolio company of RoundTable," Vanguard acquired the assets of Medical Instruments Technology, a Utah-based medical device reprocessor. This acquisition added cardiac retractors, cardiac stabilizers, curved arthroscopic shavers, and coated orthopedic blades to what we were marketing and selling as our "reprocessing service portfolio."

Then we received a request for a meeting from the office of Phil Frappaolo, who was the deputy director for the FDA's Office of Compliance, Center for Devices and Radiological Health. This came as a surprise, but it certainly didn't provoke suspicion or even very much curiosity.

I wasn't unduly concerned as I sat across from Phil in his FDA office. A man whom I both genuinely liked and respected, Phil hadn't gotten this high in the agency without having experience, expertise, and an acute knowledge of how to navigate government bureaucracies. Phil was a person of great integrity, so when he said with some degree of hesitation, "There's pressure on us, Chuck," I knew that whatever the pressure was and wherever it was being directed from were weighing heavily on him.

"The FDA is going to have to do something—take action," Phil continued. I thought, *The other guys don't care about what you're doing until you start drinking their beer and dancing with their women.*

"We're going to have to take two of your products off the market."

sequential compression device and suture packs, I was thinking, as I did the mental math. *We can take the hit.* But I knew. Instinctively, I *knew* that the Big Dogs weren't coming off that porch once again only to stop at the fence line. If they were being forced to come out into the field, they were doing so in order to head for their surgical lair, where the costliest medical devices are found.

"Scalpels," Phil said.

Oh, shit. I knew what was coming next.

"And trocars."

We're done.

Literally any other two devices would have been less damaging. Electric scalpels and trocars were the two most profitable products in the Vanguard product line.

As I continued to sit there—stunned, blindsided by the cunning nature of the Big Dogs' admittedly impressive blitzkrieg—Phil sought eye contact with me. When he was sure I was not just looking at him but actually processing his words, he slowly raised his eyes and lifted his chin toward the ceiling. Even in my daze, it was clear that Phil was signaling his role as the unfortunate messenger of a dictate that had come from upstairs. Phil's body language also made it clear that he didn't agree with the decision. But the FDA needed to throw the Big Dogs a bone—one that had a lot of meat on it. Our meat!

This was a move that was so political, it might have even originated with FDA Commissioner McClellan himself. The fact that none of us had seen it coming was shocking. The fact that I was the only person to know about it was personally devastating.

"You'll get them back on the market," Phil said in an attempt to reassure me. He seemed genuinely saddened by the situation.

For me, though, sadness hadn't yet registered. It would fully hit me during my flight home. A newly tightened budget meant that we'd have to make some serious trims to our operation. The sadness fully descended upon me when I had to update Joe on the meeting with Phil. The sadness intensified when we would all agree that there was no alternative to the devastating decisions we were going to be forced to make. We were looking at a loss of tens of thousands of dollars a month, an amount that easily exceeded our payroll. Tens of thousands of dollars *every single month*. I knew, despite RoundTable being in our corner and regardless of whether the revenge meted out by the Big Dogs proved temporary, we were done.

We ran the numbers over and over again, but couldn't avoid the necessary and unfortunate conclusions. Since so many of our employees had been with the company for multiple years, some going all the way back to the very beginning, a number of them had salaries commensurate with their loyalty, but not with their role or the market rate. As a result, some people were being overpaid. I was well aware of it; I'd never had a problem reflecting my appreciation financially for their efforts through some very tumultuous times. Thanks to the Big Dogs' latest move, however, if there was ever going to be a sale of the company, we had no choice but to downsize. And as the leader, I had no choice but to deliver this terrible news.

To make matters worse, around this time, Democratic senators Dick Durbin of Illinois and Ted Kennedy of Massachusetts—at the behest of the still-salivating Big Dogs— addressed the US Senate about the reuse of SUDs, expressing concern about what he called highly invasive and high-risk devices, devices that come in contact with the patient's blood or other bodily fluids. Senator Durbin introduced legislation requesting $1 million to aid the FDA in investigating the process of SUD reprocessing. This request was approved by the Senate.

Senator Durbin also asked Congress's General Accounting Office to initiate a comprehensive evaluation of the practice of reusing single-use medical devices, a report that would ultimately play politics, as is evident in the report's very title: *Reprocessed Single-Use Medical Devices: FDA Oversight Has Increased, and Available Information Does Not Indicate that Use Presents an Elevated Health Risk.*

* * *

I knew my judgment was clouded by my emotions, so I asked Joe to offer some guidance regarding which employees we had to let go. On paper, I could see that Tammy Goodell, who had taken over customer service when Marge returned home, was being overpaid for her position. Because of this she needed to be on that list of employees. What made it especially painful, was the fact that Tammy was also one of the first employees hired by Vanguard.

Having to let her and other employees go—especially at a time when they should have been able to finally feel comfortable with Vanguard's future—was heartbreaking and made me physically ill. If there had been anything else that stood even half a chance of succeeding, I would have charged at it as fast and as hard as I could. But the Big Dogs had us by the throat. Tempting as it might have been to believe that the only option was to cower and allow the Big Dog pack to rip us to shreds, we had to preserve what remained of the company that every single employee had contributed to building. I was down, but I was not out—I had never turned tail and run, and I sure as hell wasn't about to start now.

The evening before I had to go in and make the announcement, I don't think I said much to Marge. I have no trouble recalling the thoughts that careened through my mind as I lay awake and agonized into the wee hours: *I can't do this. How am I going to do this? They don't deserve this. I've let them down. What will happen to them? To their families? Do the Big Dogs not realize this is about more than money? These are people's lives!*

These weren't worries you wrestle with in the middle of the night only to see them dissipate with the rising sun. The reality of these fears became harsher in the unforgiving morning light. Marge considered a number of these employees her personal friends. She knew some of them better than I did. When she said goodbye to me, there was a pained expression on her face that I knew I wouldn't be able to shake any time soon.

I felt that my situation was akin to Caesar's 2,000 years ago at Alexandria, when he ordered his generals to burn their own ships—sending a clear message that there were no options left but for the Romans to give everything they had in enemy territory. I had to be the leader who made the decision that *we're going this way*, and communicate it to all who would continue the journey— and all who would not.

Shortly after arriving at work, I called the thirty individuals in question into the conference room. Waiting alongside me was the united front of Mac, Tony, Barb, and John, whose support bolstered me in the face of the heartbreak I was about to cause. A leader always owes an honest explanation that answers the emotionally driven concerns of the people involved. In this case, the office grapevine had taken root and the truth of the situation was already largely known.

"As you know," I began, reminded of the early difficulties I'd had with public speaking, "the FDA has taken two of our products off the market. Because of this ..."

This was the worst possible outcome. The expressions on the employees' faces reflected my own feelings about what is still without a doubt the hardest thing I have ever done in my professional life. Tammy in particular didn't say anything in response; she simply burst into tears. No one else said anything either. They watched Tammy escape into the hallway, her sobs seeming to grow louder instead of softer as she ran farther away from the conference room. If I could have joined her, I would have, but that was a journey these employees would have to make alone.

I felt the loss keenly. The person to whom employees typically came for help and support had in an instant become the person inflicting undeserved pain on them. It was soul-destroying, and for the hapless employees who gathered at my behest on that devastating morning—men and women who had come to Vanguard in need of a job—it was the end of a dream.

"I will never do that again," I said to Marge later that night as we both lay awake in bed, my own dream now a nightmarish reality.

My wife knew me well enough to not say anything. There was, after all, nothing that either of us could say to make this hurt go away.

* * *

If Vanguard's devices being pulled from the market was a sudden, violent storm, what lay beyond it took the wind out of everyone's sails. We should perhaps have been prepared for how quickly changing weather could blow in, but we discovered that there are some things beyond human control.

A call came in on a Friday morning during a round of golf. My cell phone rang while I was finishing up the ninth hole. When I answered, an anguished voice asked me a slew of disconcerting questions. Had I seen the news? A report about a terrible accident?

A woman by the name of Brenda Brown had been involved in the accident. The woman had been taken from the scene by ambulance—and it didn't look good.

Probably like everyone else, if I had seen the news, I wouldn't have paid it much attention. After all, the name Brenda Brown isn't exactly unusual. It was surely common enough that there was no way it could be Mac's wife. It wasn't possible that *Mac's* Brenda had been hit by a car at the car wash as she was pushing their baby boy in his stroller was it?

It was a tragic accident. The story I heard was also a clear testament to the love a mother has for her child. Brenda Brown had managed, just in time, to heroically push the stroller away from herself and from the out-of-control car, ensuring that her son would be unharmed.

The combination of the news report's mention of the woman's name and the description of her final act of fierce protection must have given some people pause. Several of them tried reaching out to Mac to reassure themselves that his Brenda was safely at home with their son, Darnell. When they found themselves unable to reach Mac despite numerous attempts, they started contacting each other about what was being reported. Surely someone must have heard something that rendered this terrible incident unrelated to Mac and his Brenda.

Mac remembers precious little about the day of Brenda's accident, and of the days that immediately followed it. There is, however, no doubt that he couldn't possibly have eased people's concern and told them that his Brenda was just fine—because his Brenda wasn't.

Rules are strictly followed in intensive care units, where Brenda was being treated after the accident. Even when patients are unconscious, as Brenda was, ICU personnel are necessarily unyielding when it comes to there being no more than two or three visitors allowed in a room at any one time. The nurses were kind as they communicated this rule, and gently guided people to the ICU waiting room to await further news about Brenda.

It goes without saying that the last thing that should have crossed Mac's mind while Brenda was hospitalized was informing people about what had happened, and it didn't. But someone must have been reaching out to his Vanguard family, because more and more people showed up at the hospital. The nurses kept guiding these people to the waiting room, only to return to Brenda's room and find that more people had since made their way in.

This continued throughout the day on Saturday. The nurses finally had to explain to Mac that they unfortunately couldn't accommodate all of the visitors. Yet the Vanguard family kept coming. The nurses eventually realized that it was pointless to keep moving people out to the waiting room. Everyone who had come to see Brenda was allowed to stay in the room—about thirty people in all, crowded together in sorrow and solidarity.

I'll never forget the sight of Brenda lying there as if asleep on those white hospital sheets, her shell-shocked husband at her side. I know, intellectually, that all things work together for good, but looking at Mac as he kept watch tugged at my understanding of the immutability of providence.

What I found myself thinking didn't center on grief or even on God. After everything the Vanguard family had endured together, as I looked at Brenda, I thought, *How can this be? How could this have happened?*

Mac still struggles to remember that difficult time with any clarity, but what he does remember are the words of love: "I love you, Mac," and "I love you, Brenda," and "I love you, Darnell," and all the hugs and the palpable sense of unity. It was an outpouring of support from the leaders, managers, and production line workers— the people who worked with and for Mac. Although they may have been asking themselves the kinds of questions I was, they wanted him to know that they were there for him in this place where neither he nor Brenda deserved to find themselves.

Mary Vermillion made funeral arrangements for her boss's wife without a second thought, embodying the shared belief that "We found Vanguard, but Vanguard also found us."

This beautiful thing followed Mac when he returned to work. His recollection isn't clear with regard to those early days after Brenda's passing, but he does recall me calling him about a week afterward.

"Mac," I said, "a lot of people didn't get the chance to see you at the hospital, and they would like to see you and spend some time with Darnell."

Mac replied, "Thank you, Chuck. That's really nice of them."

I don't think he realized at the time just how serious everyone was about the offer. Mac was used to laughing with these people and enjoying them on a daily basis at work. He couldn't have predicted they would want to show their care and concern for him and his young son in such an intimate way. People who worked in the facility, many of whom were from the plant floor, lined up in an open room and waited their turn to play with Darnell and to hug and talk with Mac.

They went even further by taking up a collection for Mac and Darnell. For a senior executive to have plant workers contribute their hard-earned wages and hand over an envelope of cash, out of pure love and the desire to express it in some tangible way, was astonishing to Mac. It wasn't the money. It wasn't even the time the employees had spent playing with his son and connecting with him. These people made it their standard behavior over the weeks and months that followed to come to him and ask how he and Darnell were doing, specifically checking on Darnell and requesting photos and updates of his newest skill and stage of growth attained.

For Mac, the feeling that he was among family was so strong and pervasive, it allowed him to continue working for almost another year, a meaningful time during this most meaningful period in his personal life. Mac's coworkers became an important part of his support system, and their flexibility, understanding, and ongoing expression of care and concern made it possible for him to stay for the months that he did. Mac actually found himself wanting to go to work, because he knew at work he would be cared for. More than a year after Brenda's passing, Mac was still driving almost an hour back and forth to work every day, simply because he still loved slaying dragons with his beloved colleagues.

Mac continued to travel as needed after Brenda's passing. One particular day as he prepared to leave town, Darnell, the little boy Brenda had sacrificed her life to protect, cried as he watched Mac pack. "Daddy," Darnell sobbed. "Daddy!"

The company had continued to be flexible about Mac's work and travel schedule, allowing him to take whatever time he needed to be with his son.

Darnell's sobs grew more intense. He looked up at his father and asked him, "Do you have to go?"

Mac asked himself whether he really had to go. The answer, he realized, was that he didn't. He didn't *have* to go and leave his son.

And so he didn't.

As Mac sees it, he has also never really left the people at Vanguard who, in his darkest hour, were at his side.

CHAPTER 20

AT HOME AND FREE

I have fought the good fight, I have finished the race, I have kept the faith.

— Paul the Apostle

In the war that the Big Dog Kingdom thrust upon us, I was no hero. I did, however, understand the need to wear a brave face. I knew if I didn't project confidence and composure at all times, it would signal the death knell to our employees. For this reason, I could not, would not allow what I was really feeling to show. Should the lines of exhaustion etched into my forehead or the weariness dulling my eyes be revealed to the troops, their loss of confidence in both commander and cause would serve up our surrender to the Big Dogs on a platter. To dodge the arrows fired for so many years, only to fall from a self-inflicted wound, would be unforgivable.

Yet, after losses to our forces and our resources, thanks in large part to the FDA pulling our products off the market, the wound didn't need to be deep to be capable of inflicting mortal damage. We were fewer in number. As for those of us still standing, we were bloodied, we were bruised, and we were bone-weary.

Phil was proven correct. We ended up getting electric scalpels and trocars back on the market after an interminable six months, but the forced downsizing made this victory feel hollow, as if we were raising the Vanguard flag over a battlefield that the Big Dogs had abandoned, not one on which they had been defeated. And so many of our own troops had already fallen.

Some have suggested that I am a man who finds the hunt more rewarding than the kill. Maybe it is true. Perhaps with MDUFMA, I gained the vindication I had been seeking for so long, and my personal fight should reach its end.

When RoundTable invested in Vanguard, Marge and I were able to sell some of our stock and pay off the mortgage on our house. I had made good on my promise that I would never again put my wife in the position of having to be concerned that she might lose her home. It was possible that the security had blinded me to the battle fatigue that had crept up on me and now restrained me in its vise-like grip.

Although all these possibilities impacted my mindset to a degree, none took the same toll on me as wearing a mask of leadership that had once fit so comfortably, but now felt unbearably heavy.

I recognize the irony of having been raised in a household where safety and security were determined by how successfully my father was able to keep his own mask fixed in place. My mask of "ultimate salesman" was one I kept relentlessly repositioning. As I have said before, a war is a war, no matter where it is fought. With my true feelings under constant threat of being uncovered, I was running low on fight.

Much as when I was a boy running out to the mailbox to bring the mail back to my mother before she could count to ten, at Vanguard I was still sprinting every day. What had changed was my perception that the distance was increasing commensurate with the diminishment of my strength and speed. However, if my mother had taught me anything, it was that I should never, never quit.

So I continued to be the same Chuck that people had always known and trusted—positive, determined, uncompromisingly assured. After all, leadership is both a gift and a responsibility shouldered alone. Relief, for even a moment, should be unthinkable to a leader. For any CEO, serving as the public face of the company may create feelings of confinement or a disquieting sense of inauthenticity, but neither should ever supersede the CEO's fortitude. When you're shielding a company's employees, you're not only absorbing the arrows, but you're doing so without crying out or even grimacing in pain.

Understanding the role, however, didn't make it any easier to play it. To the contrary. Indebted as I was to the employees, and with my admiration and gratitude rising as our time in the trenches continued, ensuring that the mask remained fixed was consuming more of my physical, emotional, and mental health with every passing day. Maintaining the veneer was so tiresome that if I were to fetch the mail now, I'd likely only reach the mailbox by crawling on my hands and knees. Challenging as it was, the alternative would be having no company left to guard, and that would have meant that the entire war had been a wasted effort.

I'm comfortable being described as a man of big ideas. Joe has long considered me someone whose base challenge is determining which idea I am going to pursue on any given day. To Joe, I am just that intellectually curious. During my lifetime, there have been quite a few labels applied to me, but the only one that has never sat well with me is that of "visionary." Although I'm warmed by the sentiment, I don't consider myself a visionary. I'm more comfortable with "quirky dynamo," or "Marge's husband," or even "mad genius." However, the effect that labeling has had on my professional life just cannot be downplayed.

All those years ago, I looked out of a cramped lab and saw men wearing the "salesman" label that I desperately wanted to wear myself. I worked to physically pin it to my suit, only to have my head turned by a more experienced salesman wearing the label of "independent sales rep." That proved to me that even the most impressive-sounding label has its limitations.

What it ultimately comes down to is action and verification. The reason the Big Dogs were never able to run us out of their kingdom was because they foisted accusatory, misleading, and emotion-driven labels on us that the science proved were without merit.

I've never faltered in my fervent belief that there has never been a war won on the actions or merits of the commander alone. I'm blessed to be described by others as the "founder of the SUD reprocessing industry," but not a single one of my steps was taken alone. I happened to walk ahead of others, but from my perspective I was marching shoulder to shoulder alongside a most loyal legion.

The supportive nature of the Vanguard troops was never more apparent than after we made it through our personal Battle of the Bulge, when the FDA pulled our devices from the market. Even for those employees who survived the downsizing, there was no denying that we would remain on very shaky ground for some time to come. So shaky that every remaining employee, from the plant floor all the way up to the executive team, took one unpaid day off every paycheck. Steve views this sacrifice by the employees—which didn't result in even one resignation—as a demonstration of their continued belief in the Vanguard vision.

We were all limping, but as the leader, I needed to throw my arms around every other shoulder and somehow steady and support us all. I could rely on no one, not even Marge, to take on a single ounce of the immense weight. There was an undeniable joy that came from witnessing employees who started out as Vanguard recruits forge lifelong bonds as brothers- and sisters-in-arms. But it can also be lonely, finding yourself unable to gather strength from those who would gladly offer you some of theirs. My father knew this loneliness, speaking of it when he sat beside me on my porch, before tearing up and weeping softly over his inability to keep the mask firmly affixed throughout my childhood. On that day, our peace accord was formed by my words: "It's okay, Dad. We both survived World War II."

* * *

By 2005, Vanguard reached almost $40 million in annual revenue. It takes just a glance at some of the numbers to recognize what the company achieved in thirteen years:

- Our plant grew from 1,000 to 125,000 square feet
- The number of employees grew to over 400
- We increased our product lines from one to twenty
- We started with two computers and expanded to 160
- Our original customer base of twelve swelled to 1,159
- From shipping forty-nine orders our first year, we shipped 60,000 in 2005
- Our gross sales increased from $50,000 to $35,638,500

As far as Marge and I were concerned, there were other metrics that were just as important as the hard business numbers. To the betterment of the community we served, Vanguard employees gave generously of their own time, effort, and money, including:

- Nine hundred pints of blood
- Six truckloads of personal care items for senior orphans
- Twelve thousand dollars and thirty-six hours of walking for Relay for Life/American Cancer Society
- Three thousand, six hundred and twenty-one tons of medical waste diverted from landfills
- More than one hundred tons of cardboard diverted from landfills

Yet, despite the emphasis we always placed on the good we pushed out into the community; our already battle-worn force needed to triple its effort to pump the necessary revenue into the company. Even if new blood kept enlisting on our side, we knew we would never be able to get our sales to where they needed to be. The numbers, impressive though they were, made it clear that reaching the $100 million in annual revenue needed to sell the company and return us all to safety was a shot in the dark. Herculean though our efforts would continue to be, the industry just wasn't big enough to support our target.

But if we were unrelenting, the Big Dogs were belligerent. Continuous losses of resources and troops had worn us down, this warfare of attrition inching us ever closer to the brink of collapse despite the momentous gains we had already made. Despite the erosion of our morale caused by all of the grinding, it had also worked to sharpen our understanding of the battlefield. By trimming away all but one strategy—that is, joining forces against a shared enemy—the relentless conflict helped reveal the path to a lasting victory against the Big Dogs.

If we merged with another reprocessor that had similar sales volume, the new company could quite literally get us to the doorstep of the $100 million annual revenue mark, without Vanguard having to sustain additional damage. We had always fought as rebels, but even rebels will ascribe to traditional wartime principles of mass and maneuver if a stronger force and unexpected approach could possibly restore freedom and peace.

Our first choice of a company to merge with would never have been our competitors out of Phoenix. After suing them for stealing company documents from our website, our alliance *with* Alliance in AMDR had always been an uneasy one. Both sides were willing to bite the bullet if doing so meant that AMDR would have our backs, but whereas suing Alliance was considered water under the bridge by the Vanguard executive management team, for certain employees, that water still held a few drops of bad blood.

So when I headed up to Chicago for the merger sit-down with Joe Damico and his fellow RoundTable principal Todd Warnock, it certainly wasn't Alliance's CEO, John Grotting, who was there to represent our merger company of choice. The meeting was with Brian Williams, the president of SterilMed, the third partner company in AMDR.

Expectations on both sides were that the negotiation would be smooth sailing. I personally saw this meeting as the precursor to my being able to sail off into the sunset with Marge, our mission accomplished.

What became as clear as day, however, was that when one side considers the deal a sure bet and is arrogant enough to act like nothing can jeopardize it, any deal can be killed. I'm sure if Brian had seen the horrified expression on my face, he would have realized that he should stop talking—but he was too busy talking down to

Joe and Todd, men who routinely negotiated multibillion-dollar deals, to realize how badly he was coming across. I sat watching my sailboat to freedom get battered by Hurricane Brian.

Brian and I shared a ride back to the airport. Despite my shock over how badly he'd blown the meeting—for me as much as for him—I couldn't help but ask, "So, how do you think that went?"

"Oh, it was great," a chipper Brian said. "They loved me!"

Sure they did, I thought as I looked out the taxi window at a snow-clad city.

My own winter of discontent was now all but guaranteed to continue indefinitely. I had commanded the troops and led the industry charge for fourteen years. The whole point of my trip to Chicago had been to seal the deal that would secure my freedom. The expectation was that I would return to Marge a liberated man, yet now I was more entrenched in my enlistment than ever.

The last time I had gone home to tell my wife something that I barely understood myself had been when I was forty years old and had four children ranging in age from eight to sixteen. I was now in my mid-fifties and those children were all adults, some with children of their own. For the first time since my service in the Air Force, it was supposed to be just Marge and me—two scrappers who could face any headwind together. As I stared blankly out the airplane window, I saw nothing ahead of me—ahead of us—but a horizon that looked like it stretched to infinity.

* * *

On my cell phone's home screen is a photo of Marge and me on a vacation we took in the Cayman Islands after I stepped down from Vanguard. I told my wife that we were now living on her time, and I meant it.

The photo is one that my children have struggled reconciling after our many years of trials and battles. In it, I'm sitting on a jet ski with Marge behind me. There's no doubt that it's Millennial Chuck who's riding that jet ski with Marge smiling broadly, happy to be along for the ride, just enjoying the moment.

Sometime earlier, in true Chuck fashion, I made the mistake of buying Marge an expensive diamond ring to celebrate, in the belief that she would say something more than "It's very nice, Chuck," and snap the box closed, never again to be reopened. I should have known that no thirty-thousand-dollar version of the pickup lines I used on that dusty road in Crete could ever express my gratitude to her for being my partner in marriage, parenthood, and faith.

What is meaningful to both of us is, in God's providence, we created a family saga, bound with coworkers who pulled together through the years to build a company, the vision and work of which has made the world a better place. Vanguard upholds Dave Kohler's adage: "Business success doesn't matter much if we can't say we left the world a better place than we found it." We now gladly say that our family legacy has had an international impact, well worth all the time spent in struggles and trials along the way.

After all, everything eventually comes to its preordained end. A person could be forgiven for assuming that I was in retreat when I spoke to all of the expectant faces looking at me with varying degrees of apprehension and fear with these words: "What I ask from you is that you show John Grotting the same allegiance you have always shown me."

In making this request, I was doing so with no mask obscuring my vision. In this world, I know that I own nothing. I am simply a manager of the things entrusted to me for a short time. By passing the CEO torch, Vanguard and Alliance could merge as Ascent Healthcare Solutions under a single commander. The objective remained unchanged, but joining forces made it easier to quell future skirmishes with the Big Dogs and ensure that ours would be a resounding victory for the ages.

With John stepping up to take command of the troops I had been immensely honored to lead, I had in fact accomplished my mission. A man who needed a job found a future and left behind him a legacy. I was going home!

* * *

Without the war with the Big Dogs and the healing power I experienced afterward at home with my wife, I don't know that I would have realized there's only so much recuperating you can do on the couch before a familiar itch creeps back in, and you find yourself once again mulling over one idea or another and thinking, *How hard can it be?*

Epilogue

On November 30, 2009, Stryker Corp, a major medical technology company, announced its acquisition of Ascent Healthcare Solutions, Inc.

Ascent had been formed by the 2005 merger of Vanguard Medical Concepts and Alliance Medical Corporation. At the time of the acquisition, it had nine hundred employees and reprocessing facilities in Phoenix, Arizona, and Lakeland, Florida, and provided services to 1,800 hospitals and group purchasing organizations throughout North America. Ascent became a division of Stryker, operating under the MedSurg group of businesses, and would continue to be known as Ascent Healthcare Solutions.

In announcing the acquisition, Stryker CEO Stephen P. MacMillan said that with FDA regulations, reprocessing and remanufacturing has become one of the most impactful programs in use at hospitals, allowing for significant costs savings to the health care system. Additionally, Ascent's programs allow its partner hospitals to divert thousands of pounds of medical waste from landfills while simultaneously redirecting substantial financial resources to patient care quality initiatives.

Stryker paid $560 million in cash for Ascent Healthcare Solutions.

Testimonies from the Vanguard Family

I was lucky enough to get to ride the Vanguard rocket! Chuck gave a twenty-one-year-old kid a chance, and we both never looked back. We had so many good times that even the bad times were *good* times. My relationship with Chuck and all of the Maseks altered the course of my life, personally and professionally. Coworkers truly became family. I met my wife through a Vanguard employee. We all learned and grew together as the company flourished. As Chuck led us, I learned that taking the high road *every time* really does lead to high altitudes...one of the many lessons I have carried with me for the rest of my life. At Vanguard all of us knew we were part of something special; we just didn't know that we would never be able to duplicate the Vanguard experience again.

- Steve Bernardo

I have so many wonderful memories of my time working at Vanguard, but one is very special to me. As a product manager, I worked closely with the outside sales reps. Our New York rep, Jack Fox, called me one day and said he had a very special request from one of his contacts at Mercy Hospital. The contact was connected with an organization called the Niger Fistula Foundation, which provides medical care for women in Niger who have childbirth-related complications such as obstetric fistulas. Left untreated, the women will develop severe infections and suffer much pain from the fistula.

Jack's contact was requesting certain surgical items that they could carry over to help in the foundation's efforts. Jack sent me the list to see if we could help. After researching our finished goods overstock inventory, I was surprised to see that we indeed had a good amount of what they were requesting. So, after clearing it with my boss, I began working with several people to pull and collect what I could for the foundation. I boxed everything up and sent it on to the contact at Mercy. Several weeks passed before I received an email from Jack with an attached picture of a man in a lab coat sitting at a desk with the box I had sent with a big smile on his face. It was good to know that we could help, even in just a small way. I felt very grateful to be a part of an organization that was not only okay with helping, but encouraged it, both internally and externally.

Several more weeks passed, and Jack called to say that I would be receiving a small box but not to open it until I called him. So, when I got the mysterious box, I gave Jack a call. He told me to sit down and open it. In the box was a bronze statue of a woman on her knees, arms raised and hands on her head. I immediately thought of the suffering of these women and was moved to tears. But Jack then said that they had made this statue for me. It was a woman praising God for relief from her pain. Needless to say, I was speechless. I still treasure the figurine and display it in my home. I have shared the story with my children and grandchildren as an encouragement to always look for the wonderful opportunities to help others whenever you can.

- *Vicky Kennedy*

My time at Vanguard Medical Concepts was some of the best in my life, both personally and professionally! Not only were the people fun and talented to work with, but we had a mission that few people get to participate in during their lifetime…creating a new industry. When you have customers that act more like fellow employees, who cheer you on and help to ensure the survival of the industry, you know you have started something very special. Everyone felt that "Reprocessing was the Right Thing to Do!"

Vanguard Medical Concepts consistently delivered on its promise to deliver safe medical devices at half the cost. We saved the hospitals millions, patients even more, and we ultimately created 400+ jobs for our employees—something I remain excited about to this day!

Vanguard instituted many firsts in our industry to win our argument that reprocessing was safe and the science was sound. We tracked every medical device we reprocessed with a barcode, ensuring it didn't outlive its useful life; millions and millions of devices were safely reprocessed without incident. We developed relationships with regulatory authorities to verify safe collection of the devices to ensure public safety. We developed sophisticated logarithms that could accurately determine our customers' savings. We developed device testing that matched or exceeded quality-control processes used by the original device manufactures, and we upgraded our sterile packaging to meet or exceed original device manufacturers'. Vanguard's reprocessing of single-use devices reduced tons of waste going into America's landfills. We have a lot to be proud of!

-   *Mark Salomon*

Two words come to mind as I reflect on my decade at Vanguard Medical Concepts: commitment and fulfillment. I learned well at Vanguard that these two words are positively correlated. As one increases, so does the other. At Vanguard, commitment was spending all night performing validations of cleaning and sterilization processes. Commitment was working weekends, holidays, and everything in between to not only keep growing but to keep food on the family's table. It was the generation of scientifically grounded data which shielded us against the misleading and outright false claims by large original medical equipment manufacturers who put profit ahead of their customers and the environment. Commitment was readily observable across all levels of the organization. It was woven into the fabric of the team and our united struggle to succeed against seemingly insurmountable odds.

The fulfillment of my experience at Vanguard wasn't fully appreciated until I shared these countless memories of commitment with my mentor and dear friend Doug Stante during his final days. The bonds we forged through the trials of our shared time at Vanguard ultimately led me to this conclusion: fulfillment in one's career, as in one's life, is experienced in the enduring and powerful relationships we create with other people. Experience, skill sets, expertise, and professionalism were all byproducts of time spent at Vanguard. Yet it was the people who worked for something larger than themselves and placed more value on one another than business goals and objectives that has endured all these years. I am thankful to have firsthand experience of how a committed team can realize an expansive vision and in so doing achieve fulfillment in the careers and relationships they form.

- Seth Masek

Chuck introduced Vanguard to me in the early 1990s. At that time, I was involved with my own company, serving the Northern California marketplace. My business partner (Jim Compagno) and I decided to look at our market and see what opportunities existed. We found that many hospitals were already doing some kind of reprocessing of disposables, on a limited basis, and with the right marketing approach we could have a place in their facilities.

So, we decided to take on Vanguard. Oh boy, what a ride! Because of the need for medical-waste reduction in hospitals, and the desire to save money, you would have thought it was a no-brainer. But the original manufacturers, politicians, and clinical pushback made it difficult, mounting resistance came from every angle.

But the science in most cases prevailed.

Our success came from the fact that Vanguard had an executive management team, sales team, and support staff that were totally committed and worked extremely well together. We genuinely liked each other! It was fun!

Unquestionably, my most challenging, and at the same time enjoyable, ten years.

- *Mike Mayry*

What was Vanguard? A pioneer in the medical device reprocessing industry? The brainchild of a gifted, daring, and driven young entrepreneur? A "for-profit" entity with the goal of rewarding those fortunate enough to be investors and stockholders? Well, yes, it was all of these things. But for me, too, Vanguard was the very body of individuals who were in a sense the "fabric" of the company itself—a group of individuals interacting almost as a family, with a workplace chemistry often longed for but only rarely attained; a group of individuals sharing lives, laughter, and tears. Every individual was seemingly a bit *off center* compared at least to the individual standing next to them, but worked together to make a seemingly *perfect center* between them—kind of like … family.

I had been a hotel manager with a history of staffing and building teams in that industry, but somewhat in search of a new avenue professionally, and raising a family when Chuck Masek initially began talking to me about the possibility of a position with his new young company. He emphasized the time was not yet—the company was more vision at that point. When the time finally came, he told me he was looking for someone to help build a team of employees, but someone who would clearly need to be willing to wear other hats while the company was still small. In addition to HR, I would at least for the time being be responsible for the warehouse, facilities, purchasing, etc. And the pay would be considerably less than what I was accustomed to. I immediately accepted. Considering the opportunity then and now, it was an answer to prayer and a God-brought opportunity.

- *Henry Philpot*

Being involved with Vanguard Medical Concepts was the most exciting, rewarding, worthwhile professional venture of my life.

I was part of a team that took absolutely nothing and not only created a product but an entire industry. The magic of the Vanguard experience for me was the tight-knit family we created, all banding together to reach the same goal. In spite of so many odds and foes as large and powerful as they come, we prevailed! Trite, but it was a true David and Goliath story. We were David, and the original equipment manufacturers and the US government were Goliath. Our mighty stone was the commitment and support of our hospital customers, who shared in the belief that responsible medical device reprocessing was the "right thing to do."

I have so many memories, but I believe one of the most vivid and telling is of our first visit from the two top executives from the young company. Scott Wait, my partner, and I had worked tirelessly to lay the groundwork in the largest hospital system in St. Louis. Scott and I were not new to medical sales, or to the St. Louis market. We both had recently come off successful careers with a major medical company. We developed significant interest with the director of purchasing and were granted an audience for Chuck Masek and Bill Frisbey to meet with him about our company and service. At that time, Vanguard was operating in an extremely small storefront in Plant City, Florida, with a handful of employees.

- *Mary Vermillion*

I will never forget the look you gave me, Chuck, when I said in front of Marge that Vanguard was a "fragile business." I thought for a second that I was about to go over the wrought-iron railing of the New Orleans restaurant we were drinking at—er, I mean *eating* at. Thanks for forgiving me back then for saying those words in front of Marge; my timing was wrong, no doubt caused by beer, but wrong, nonetheless. The good news is that it is now a laughable moment.

- *Scott Wait*

Chuck, I'll never forget the sales call you and I made to the hospital in Milwaukee to lay out the Vanguard Plus program. We met with the CFO and the VP of purchasing and I laid out the program to them. Barely a second had gone by when the CFO pointed to the door and repeatedly said, "Get out!" You and I looked behind us to see who he was talking to, only to realize it was us he was kicking out. We never did figure out what set him off, but we laughed about it for years. You said it was the only sales call you ever made where you got thrown out on your ear.

Thanks for the great opportunity.

- *Jeff Schroeder*

My time at Vanguard provided all my first "real-world" business experiences that I have carried with me and built upon throughout my professional career. While it did not feel like a positive at the time, I would say the frequent exposure to the FDA investigations and all the regulatory challenges that we overcame as a result of pioneering the reprocessing industry provided some of the most valuable training experiences I have continued to benefit from in all work experiences since.

- Robin Wilson

I started with Vanguard in 1997 and had a great run. In 2004, my life changed when I went through a divorce. I was in Chuck's office talking through my life changes when he offered for me to stay in his home. Of course, I wasn't going to take him up on his offer, but then he explained that he and Marge had built a garage apartment for their children to use and offered me its use. I stayed there for nearly a year. I learned later that this apartment is really the "Masek home for wayward boys," as I was not the first to stay there and probably not the last. Marge and Chuck took me into their family. The three of us spent many nights dining together and watching the news. Marge and Chuck have had a profound influence in my life. Their Christian beliefs shine in their actions and deeds, and I will forever be grateful for their love and care for me and Team Vanguard.

Fast forward to today. I am experiencing some health issues that will require me to move back to Florida for a few months. Almost before I could finish telling Chuck about my situation, he once again offered to help me with accommodations during my stay for treatments.

I love you, Marge and Chuck.

- Dave McElhaney

The majority of my Vanguard career was spent working for and learning from Steve Bernardo on the IT side. It was in that capacity that I was responsible for multiple activities from routine computer maintenance to helping build the Vanguard website with

Mark Salomon. One of my daily tasks was to monitor and maintain the sales portal of the website. In this portal, Steve would feed sales figures along with important and sensitive documents. This was generally a routine task with light activity on the sales portal.

One day I noticed a spike on the portal and my heart jumped with glee to see that, finally, someone was utilizing the full potential of the portal. I quickly pulled up the numbers and the geolocation data and ran the three steps it took to get to Steve's office, asking him, "Which of our sales reps is based in Phoenix?" Steve seemed perplexed and told me that we didn't have a sales rep in Phoenix, but our largest competitor, Alliance, was there. We looked at each other, confused for a second, then my heart sank. Not only was the joy of having the sales portal finally being seen as the masterpiece it was ripped from me, but it looked like the portal had been pilfered of its sensitive material.

I only heard bits and pieces after we reported the malfeasance, until I heard that there would be a lawsuit and I was to be deposed. When the day came, I met with our lawyer, Dave Galloway, and the first and only thing he told me before heading into the meeting was "Do not say more than you have to." This could be hard for me. I walked into the room and there sat the opposing counsel and their IT consultant, who was at least two decades my senior. My immediate thought was that maybe having a teenager be deposed was not the best idea.

The deposition went along mind-numbingly for what seemed like hours (but was probably minutes) until the lawyer across the table asked how we could prove the files were downloaded and not viewed. I sat there, remembering Dave's advice. I wanted to enter into a diatribe, explaining the question's invalidity and also telling my counterpart on the other side of the table that he should know better than to let that question be asked. I didn't. Instead, I leaned back and quietly explained the situation to Dave. He smirked as he understood, and then he answered the question on my behalf, in lawyer jargon that sounded much more polite than what I was eager to say.

After that, I was confident Vanguard would prevail in this dispute.

- *Nathan Masek*

My time at Vanguard was the most rewarding of my career. Vanguard was truly a team environment that focused on business and family! We worked hard to drive revenues and to achieve our goals, but we did so in an environment of mutual respect and inclusion. Our leadership solicited everyone's input to ensure we considered all markets and all points of view. Once the plan was formalized, we leveraged everyone's talent and relationships to meet the team objectives. This process ensured that all team members were committed to and invested in a mutually beneficial outcome. Vanguard was a true partnership and a family environment that helped create lifelong friendships—an environment that since my departure I have yet to experience again.

- *Bryan Eckard*

Vanguard meant so much to me, I don't know where to begin. I believe the most important thing was the relationships developed among managers, upper management, and customers. Managers shared what was successful and what was not. Upper management learned to give us leeway to get the job done. And customers, well, they became customers if we were successful. To this day, I believe we maintain a lot of these relationships.

Several things made me successful at Vanguard: the relationships, the sharing with managers and with upper management, the freedom to do what we thought was necessary, and the customers, who taught us we were more educators than salesmen.

My two biggest successes were growing a region from $170,000 a year to a $1 million a month. My second was taking a customer to a million-dollar-a-year customer.

- *Mike Rovnak*

My first impression of Chuck Masek and Vanguard was a lasting one. I couldn't believe how evangelical or committed this "mad scientist" was about helping hospitals from an environmental as well as a financial perspective. He had a million ideas and talked as fast as a speeding bullet, but the common thread in everything that he said was that he seemed to deeply care for people and wanted to make a difference.

Many months passed, and I visited Chuck again; it was as if the hands of time had stood still. He picked up exactly where he left off. The energy, the exuberance, and the passion were all there about the science behind reprocessing and the team that he had assembled to "change the market."

What I grew to respect and really appreciate about Chuck, over the years that we worked together, was that personal financial success meant very little to both him and Marge. He was driven by a burning desire to simply make things better. In my forty-three-plus years in health care and going on twenty years in private equity, I can honestly say that Chuck is "one of a kind," and I for one am far better off for knowing him.

- *Joe Damico*

A period that stands out for me as a turning point at Vanguard was when we temporarily lost several 510(k)s and had to stop reprocessing our highest-value products for a period of time. The company was under great financial pressure and was faced with some hard choices to keep the business afloat. Ultimately, we decided to go to a four-day workweek for every person in the business, including all salaried employees.

Our salaried employees, including the executive leadership, all agreed to a pay cut equivalent to a four-day week, and were allowed to take that fifth day off work. Through all of this, we did not lose any employees. Everybody stuck with us through this difficult period. That is when I knew we had something special!

- *Tony O'Neill*

My time at Vanguard remains the toughest yet most rewarding and fulfilling business experience of my career. We were a group of people who, under tremendous pressure from outside forces, were forged first into an extremely high-performance team made up of exceptional individuals, then into a caring family! The most powerful impression that remains with me to this day is how in the face of the constant risk of annihilation we had fun and *loved* working together every day! It was truly an exceptional experience.

Thanks, Chuck, for allowing me to be a part of the ride. Through it all, it was your soaring intellect and unwaveringly principled leadership that drew the finest people to Vanguard, then motivated them to do something special. Your boundless energy and faith in us made this happen. We absolutely couldn't have done this without you as our leader!

Vanguard remains an unforgettable experience that will always hold a very special place in my life.

- *Mac Brown*

I started as a Vanguard customer but then came to work for the company from June 2002 until May 2007.

Some memories include testifying in Chicago, all the wonderful educational experiences with hospital staff, working with the sales reps, and of course all the wonderful people I met and worked with at Vanguard.

- *Deb Haley*

When I reflect on my time at Vanguard, there is not one specific memory that comes to mind. Rather, when I think of Vanguard, it is the people I recall most. Our team worked hard to achieve a common vision. We maintained focus and discipline through the challenges associated with an evolving business. Our team appreciated laughter and celebrated the many successes. The people, and the corresponding friendships, made Vanguard a special experience.

- *Barbara Sullivan*

ACKNOWLEDGMENTS

I'd like to thank Erin McKnight and Terry Glaspey for their help in breathing life into the writing of Vanguard's extraordinary story.